MW00973065

Teaching

a

Preschooler

to

Read

RK

Royce-Kotran Publishing
Boston

Teaching

a Preschooler

to Read

Phonics for Parents

and Other Care-Givers

Stephen Parker

Copyright © 2017 by Stephen Parker

Royce-Kotran Publishing
Boston, MA

All rights reserved.

No part of this book may be reproduced in any form by any electronic or mechanical means (including photocopying, recording, or information storage and retrieval) without written permission from the publisher.

Printed and bound in the United States of America.

Last digit is the edition number: 9 8 7 6 5 4 3 2 1

ISBN 978-0-9994585-0-1

Library of Congress Control Number: 2017957436

Contents

Preparation for Teaching

The Reading Program

Appendices

Introduction

I would not have written this book but for the plight of my first child, Kate. As she approached her second birthday, she chattered constantly; the trouble was, my wife and I couldn't understand most of what she said. When we realized that trying to learn *her* language was not helping the situation, and perhaps making it worse, we decided to get her some professional help. But after five months of weekly meetings with a speech therapist, Kate showed little progress.

Frustrated that nothing seemed to be helping, I sat down with her and our collection of colorful plastic letters. She could already identify most of the letters, so I started to teach her something new: letters symbolize specific sounds. I kept it simple: S says "sss," U says "uh," N says "nnn." Once she mastered a half-dozen or so letter/sound relationships, I showed her how she could take a simple three-letter word like SUN, blend the sounds of the 3 letters together, and thus pronounce the word and recognize it. Words she learned to read in this manner – words built from the ground up – she spoke flawlessly.

Much encouraged, the two of us kept at it. Each time she learned a new letter/sound relationship, I would show her that letter in some simple words and then help, as needed, with the blending of the word's sounds. I started to write individual words she could read (MOM, MESS, KISS, MAN, CAT) on index cards so we could daily review them. Within 6 months her speech problems vanished and our collection of index cards grew into a stack a foot tall. By her third birthday, she could read any one-syllable word which had only short vowels. By the time we completed our letter/sound studies, she was in her mid-threes and she could read any age-appropriate book independently. She went on to read all of Mary Pope Osborne's *Magic Tree House* books, and most of Carolyn Keene's *Nancy Drew Mysteries*, before kindergarten.

Kate's younger twin brothers did not have her speech problems. Still, seeing what had been possible with Kate, I decided to teach them to read as well. Starting around the time of their 2nd birthday, I went through the process again, this time with two enthusiastic students, neither one shy about correcting his sibling's pronunciations. Both boys were reading children's books independently by their early-threes.

* * * * *

That was more than a decade ago; now, all my children are in college. It seems to me that for a parent to take on a project as significant as teaching a preschooler to read, the parent must come to 4 conclusions:

- My preschooler is capable of learning to read.
- It will benefit my child to do so.
- I have (or can make) the time to teach my preschooler.
- I have the expertise to perform the task.

I may have already convinced you (if you needed it) that preschoolers are capable of reading. See Chapter 1 for why early literacy is advantageous for them. I assure you: as long as you're a reasonably competent reader yourself, you *do* have the expertise. All you need is a guide – precisely what this book provides.

If you don't make time for this project, your only alternative is to allow a local school, public or private, to do it for you. Here's one problem with that plan. Go to the web site *www.nationsreportcard.gov* and start looking through the data on the reading ability of this nation's 4th and 8th graders. You'll discover that, for the past quarter-century of nationwide testing, only 1 in 3 students was classified as a "proficient" or "advanced" reader. All the rest of the students (2 out of 3!) were classified "basic" or "below basic." In other words, 1 in 3 students is being prepared for college and for our highly competitive job market; 2 out of 3 students are barely getting by – or they're illiterate.

By taking on this project and using this book as your guide, you'll be teaching your preschooler to read *phonetically*. You'll be using the full-strength version of phonics – the version that the National Reading Panel, in its 2000 Final Report, called "Systematic Phonics" (see Chapter 3). Congress convened this group of scholars in 1997 "to assess the effectiveness of different approaches used to teach children to read." The Panel concluded: "Systematic Phonics makes a bigger contribution to children's growth in reading than alternative programs providing unsystematic or no phonics instruction."

One reason schools are doing a poor job teaching literacy is that many of them use methods other than Systematic Phonics. One such method, popular in the 80's and 90's, was called Whole Language; another, popular now, is called Balanced Literacy. It's puzzling to me that educational leaders are so resistant to Systematic Phonics. They avoid it despite the findings of the National Reading Panel, despite the poor results of their own methods, and despite the fact that written English is based on an *alphabet* in which every letter symbolizes sound.

That alphabet is one of humankind's greatest achievements. Our version of it, the modern English alphabet, consists of 26 letters, each symbolizing one or more of the 41 elemental sounds of the English language. But any alphabet, from the Greek or Latin version up to our own, enables its users to perform 2 tasks which, upon reflection, are astonishing: drawing sound on paper (spelling) and absorbing language through the eyes (reading).

By simply rearranging these 26 letters, we can depict the million spoken words of our complex language, easily and elegantly, as print. The alphabetic code (see Chapter 2) encompasses about 100 letter/sound relationships. While complex, this code is logical, and therefore teachable. To master it is to master two essential skills at once: encoding sound into text and decoding text back into sound. The Systematic Phonics program in this book will guide you as you teach your child all the intricacies of this code, in an explicit and carefully sequenced manner.

You may be wondering about the time necessary to complete this ambitious and exciting project. Can your child already identify the 52 upper and lowercase letters of the alphabet? If "no," you'll need to start with Stage 1, and this program will take about a year-and-a-half. If "yes," you can start with Stage 2 and it will take about a year. In estimating these times, I assume you'll devote about an hour per day to the task: 30-45 minutes for explicit teaching and word practice, and another 20-30 minutes for reading children's literature to your child. I know this is a considerable time commitment, but by the end of this program, your child will be on par with the best readers in any third grade across the country. Reading is a complex skill, and like any complex skill, mastering it takes time and effort.

You may also be wondering how early this reading program can begin. Here are *minimum* age guidelines: for Stage 1, focusing only on letter recognition, a child can be as young as two; for Stage 2, when reading begins, the child should be in her mid-twos. Any age older, of course, is fine.

You'll find no gimmicks in this program. There are no other workbooks to buy, no costly software, and no web sites where, for a monthly fee, you can log on. You'll need only this book, pencil and paper, blank index cards, and some magic markers. While I wrote this book primarily for parents who wish to teach a preschool child to read, it can easily be adapted to teach older children, or even adults. The method I use here, Systematic Phonics, is the most effective way to teach *anyone* to read.

A word about pronouns and inclusive language. Every time I see "his or her," "he or she," or "s/he" when I am reading, it distracts me. In this book, I freely switch back and forth between masculine and feminine pronouns. I don't know which pronoun I used more often, however, I tried not to switch in the middle of a paragraph. By alternating pronouns, I hope to include everyone.

There are 3 preliminary chapters to read if you intend to use this phonics program with your child. In Chapter 1, I discuss multiple reasons for teaching your preschooler to read. In Chapter 2, I discuss the coded nature of both reading and spelling, along with the one skill you'll need to acquire *before* beginning the program. In Chapter 3, I discuss, in some detail, the Systematic Phonics program you'll be using, and I contrast it with how reading is taught in many of our local schools.

To teach reading to a preschooler you need time, patience, humor, and a sound strategy. This book provides the strategy; the other items are up to you. After food, shelter, and love, I believe the gift of literacy is the most important gift you can give a child. Best wishes as you begin this rewarding project – you'll never regret doing it!

Stephen Parker
November 2017

Table 1
The 41 Elemental Sounds of English

17 Vowel Sounds

Name of the Sound	Notation for the Sound	Words Using the Sound
short A	/a/	ax, apple, cat
long A	/A/	alien, labor, date
short E	/e/	egg, bed, pet
long E	/E/	evil, begin, she
short I	/i/	in, kiss, with
long I	/I/	idea, hiker, mild
short O	/o/	ox, not, bother
long O	/O/	ocean, omit, go
short U	/u/	up, gum, mud
	/oo/	good, book, wool
	/ew/	new, stew, brew
	/oy/	boy, toy, oyster
	/ow/	cow, allow, how
	/aw/	law, hawk, awful
r-controlled A	/ar/	arm, cart, shark
r-controlled E	/er/	clerk, term, nerd
r-controlled O	/or/	for, corn, sport

24 Consonant Sounds

Name of the Sound	Notation for the Sound	Words Using the Sound
	/b/	bat, bird
	/d/	dad, deck
	/f/	fun, fast
	/g/	gift, girl
	/h/	hat, hope
	/j/	jet, jam
	/k/	kiss, keep
	/l/	lip, last
	/m/	mom, most
	/n/	nut, note
	/p/	pet, past
	/r/	rug, reach
	/s/	sun, surf
	/t/	top, time
	/v/	van, vine
	/w/	win, went
	/y/	yard, yellow
	/z/	zip, zest
	/ch/	chip, chase
unvoiced SH	/sh/	ship, sheep
voiced SH	/SH/	Asia, vision
	/ng/	king, song, bang
unvoiced TH	/th/	thin, thrift, path
voiced TH	/TH/	this, then, those

For a discussion of these sounds, see Chapters 2 and 3.
For a summary of the entire English code, see appendices P and Q.

Chapter 1
Why Teach a Preschooler to Read?

I suspect many of us underestimate the intellectual capabilities of preschoolers. We're amazed at how quickly toddlers master their primary speaking language, and if offered, a second language as well. Yet most of us do not teach our children to read. Instead, we rely on our local schools to perform this vital task for us, starting in kindergarten or first grade. For multiple reasons, I believe this is a mistake.

First, *early reading instruction enhances the child's brain development*. By "early reading instruction" I mean teaching letter recognition during the child's twos, and starting actual reading instruction by the late twos or early threes. Brain development in early childhood defies belief. A baby is born with all the brain neurons she'll ever have: around 100 billion. Each one of those 100 billion neurons is capable of forming thousands of links (synapses) with other neurons, giving the brain over 100 trillion synaptic connections.[1]

The synapses already present at birth govern the use of the five senses and such automatic processes as heart rate, breathing, blood pressure, sleeping, and digestion.[2] Most brain *development*, however, takes place after birth, through the creation, activation, and use of new synapses brought about by the child's environment and early experiences.[3] A loving and intellectually stimulating environment leads to greater brain development; an abusive or neglectful environment results in less brain development. Biology need not be destiny. The child's early environmental experiences are literally "brain-shaping." Intelligence is not wholly fixed at birth by genetics; it "also depends on the environmental experiences the child is exposed to on a consistent basis."[4]

The first three years of life are especially important in this process of brain development. The brain nearly triples in size during the first year of life – and by age 3, it has 85 percent of its future adult weight. The increase in weight is not due to growth in brain cells, but to synaptic growth and to myelination.[5] During this time, synaptic formation occurs at an astonishing rate: up to 10 billion connections per day.[6] The 14-18 hours of sleep infants and small children need each day is required to preserve metabolic energy for this enormous task of brain development. "In these earliest years, the way information flows through the brain's structures, and gets processed, is largely established. These pathways and structures will be used and reused as learning continues throughout life."[7]

Synaptic density reaches a peak in the child's third year of life at around one quadrillion connections, *double* the number she'll have as an adult. After this critical three-year period, the brain gradually begins to discard unneeded and unused synapses through a normal process called "pruning." The synapses not pruned are those she strengthens though repeated use.[8]

This excess production of synapses during the first three years of life makes the brain particularly responsive to external stimuli. During this period, the child can learn more easily and more efficiently than she'll be able to learn at any other time in her life. Her brain acts like a "black hole," voraciously sucking in novel information and new experiences. This helps explain why young children can easily learn to speak a second language, while older children and adults often find this task disagreeable and difficult.

To be sure, it's never too late for a parent to influence the wiring of a child's brain – certainly not at age 3, and not even at age 13. "The brain has a remarkable, lifelong capacity to reorganize itself in response to the information it receives from its environment. Researchers call this *neural plasticity* and it takes place at all ages... A child of any age benefits from the ABC's."[9] What is true, however, is the older one gets, the longer it takes the brain to "rewire" in response to what it experiences.

There is no make-or-break time for teaching a child to read. However, given the phenomenal way the brain develops in the preschool years, it seems to me a more appropriate title for this chapter might be: "Why *Not* Teach a Preschooler to Read?" Why would a parent *not* add reading instruction to all the other new experiences which are creating, activating, and strengthening synaptic connections in the child's young brain?

Beyond enhanced brain development, what other reasons are there for teaching a preschooler to read? Let's suppose it is indeed possible for a parent to teach their 3, 4, or 5-year old how to read, and that doing so will take about a year. Alternatively, the parent can leave this task to the local school. Let's assume that school will perform this task competently, and it will take the school's teachers 3 years (grades K, 1, and 2) to get your child, by age 8, to the point of reading independently. My question is this: what benefits accrue to a child who has a 3 to 5-year head start in a skill as fundamental as reading? Well, once a child can read independently, he becomes capable of both self-entertainment and self-learning. Preschoolers who can read, quickly become passionate readers. They spend hours with children's books, allowing those books to transport them to other real and fantasy worlds. Their brains are constantly stimulated by their reading, an activity *they* now control. Their knowledge, fluency, vocabulary, and self-confidence grow exponentially.

If you grant the gift of literacy to your preschooler, you might suppose his peers will eventually catch up to him once he goes to school. This is not the case. Instead, a phenomenon, known variously as "Cumulative Advantage," or "The Matthew Effect," starts to unfold. The reference is to a verse in the Bible (Matthew 25:29) which has, over time, become a maxim: "the rich get richer while the poor get poorer." The effect, studied in such diverse fields as science, economics, sociology, psychology, and education,[10] can occur when an advantage, conferred at the beginning of some process, becomes a resource that leads to skills and opportunities – skills and opportunities which in turn produce even further relative gains over time.

It's not difficult to see how the Matthew Effect would apply to an early reader. A child given such an advantage makes an early transition from "learning to read" to "reading to learn." His vocabulary explodes. His independent reading skill provides opportunities in other subjects as he begins amassing knowledge on his own. He spends little time and effort, relative to his peers, in word recognition, leaving more time and energy for comprehension and higher-level thinking. Due to his reading skill, he is regarded as being "smart," and consequently, he receives lots of praise and attention from meaningful adults. His self-confidence expands, and his teachers have lofty expectations for him – expectations that serve to propel him along even further and faster. To keep such positive feedback flowing, he is motivated to read even more, thus assuring an ever-accelerating cycle of effort and reward. If you decide to teach your preschooler how to read, the head start you give him will not only persist over time, it will grow, and it will have enormous implications in all his future academic pursuits. It is a gift that will last a lifetime.

A third reason for giving your child an early start in reading is this: if you don't do it, then by default, you'll be relying on your local school to perform this critical task for you. However, there is serious risk with this strategy: many of the nation's schools, public and private, do a poor job teaching literacy. You'll be playing a form of Reading Roulette, hoping your local school is not using the latest iteration of a teaching method that has repeatedly failed millions of children. That method, generically called Whole Word, has been around for close to a century. In the 80's and 90's it was called "Whole Language," now it's known as "Balanced Literacy" or "The Balanced Approach."

Consider the fact that nearly 50% of American adults are either illiterate or they are functionally illiterate.[11] That represents about 90 million Americans who can't read the Sunday newspaper or enjoy a good novel. Recently, the National Center for Education Statistics evaluated the reading level of 8th graders across the nation. It found that 34% were proficient (or better) at reading.[12] Stated differently, 66% of 8th graders (2 out of 3!) were *deficient* readers. What academic future does a student have if he is struggling with reading in 8th grade?

I just outlined three reasons for parents to make it a priority to teach their own child to read before sending them off to school. Maybe you're convinced, but you doubt you have the time. This time question is a real concern for many families, especially if both parents work or if the household is run by a single parent. In such cases, your only choice may be to do what you can, in whatever time you *do* have. Perhaps more can be done on weekends than on weeknights when everyone is tired. The pace is yours to set in this reading program. What does it matter if it takes 2, or even 3 years? Your preschooler will still benefit if you choose to instruct her yourself.

If your child is not yet 2 years old, what can you do now, specifically, to help prepare him for this reading program? First, don't become stressed about it. Do what any responsible parent does for her child, whether she intends to teach reading or not:

- Spend lots of one-on-one time playing with him and cuddling him.
- Respond promptly and predictably to his needs.
- Speak to him, early and often.
- Sing to him.
- Read to him.

In short, *interact positively* with your child. All the above activities significantly contribute to synapse creation and to the wiring of a healthy brain. While these activities fall under the category of "common sense" for most parents, here are some useful facts you may *not* already know.

"The effect of language spoken to the child cannot be over-emphasized. There is a direct correlation between the number of words heard by a child during early development, and the cognitive abilities of the child even into the late preschool years. The more words a child hears, the faster she or he will learn language."[13] The time to start speaking to your baby is Day One. "From the very first moments of life, early brain structures begin to change, wiring up according to the language heard in each child's particular environment."[14] Your newborn won't verbally respond to your speech for most of her first year of life. Nonetheless, by speaking to her, you are literally *shaping her brain*, causing synapses to grow and to strengthen. Her brain processes every word you say, and the 41 sounds of the English language that you articulate, quickly become deeply rooted in her brain. (I've listed these sounds in Table 1 in the front of this book.)

At birth, a baby's brain is genetically capable of discerning the unique sounds of *any* of the world's languages. Each language has its own cadence, rhythms, stress patterns, and intonations. Collectively, these characteristics are called *prosody*. The prosodic pattern of English is termed "stress-time," meaning certain syllables receive more stress, and are held for a longer time, than other syllables. In the first month of life, a newborn "is capable of discriminating different prosodic patterns and can recognize utterances in their native language from those in languages with different prosodic patterns... By 5 months, infants can discriminate their own language from others with the same prosodic patterns."[15] By 10-12 months of age, this amazing ability on the part of the infant brain, to discriminate the sounds of any language, has vanished – the unused synapses have been pruned away – leaving the child primed and ready for speech, in his particular native language.[16]

So, during your child's first months of life, speak frequently throughout the day. You are reinforcing the prosody and the sounds of English in her brain. It doesn't matter what you talk about – you can read Tolstoy aloud or you can simply narrate your day. Whenever the child is alert, interact with her, make eye contact, respond to her facial expressions and her sounds with your own. In her book, *Bright from the Start*, Dr. Jill Stamm devotes an entire chapter to the importance of speaking to a child, from birth, if a parent wishes to enhance the child's brain development. "The more words spoken in the home, the higher the IQ scores were at age three – regardless of socioeconomic status. By age 4, children in the language-richest homes had heard *thirty-two million more words* than those in the more language-impoverished homes. Kids who are exposed to more language, from birth, wind up, on average, smarter... Talk may be cheap, but for young children it is priceless."[17]

At around 4 months of age, you can start to supplement your speaking with a daily ritual of reading to your child as you hold her. She can now comfortably sit in your lap, and she has the visual acuity to see the pages clearly. Start with colorful cloth and cardboard books. Read expressively, adding your own story line and questions to the simple plot. Do lots of pointing to characters, colors, shapes, and objects. Read the same book multiple times; the repetition is beneficial at this age. Make the reading *interactive* as she grows older and becomes capable of it. In other words, get her involved as you read: have her point to the dog, the balloon, or to other objects on the page. As she grows older still, get her to speak as you read: "What color is that balloon?" "How many animals do you see on this page?" And when she is older still, encourage her to make conjectures and discuss emotions: "Why do you think the dog did that?" "What do you think will happen next?" "How does that make you feel?"

What follows are some useful guideposts[18] as you speak and read to your child over his first two years of life. The times are only approximate.

- Age 4 months: Your baby starts responding to signals. A bottle or a breast becomes a signal to "eat."
- 5-7 months: The infant begins to respond to high-frequency words like "mommy," "daddy," and "bye-bye."
- 9 months: Babies begin to imitate adult vocalizations and they begin to use gestures to communicate.
- 12 months: The child begins to speak. These first words show the beginnings of *symbolic* thought. A spoken word, "doggie" for instance, is a symbol for the actual dog. At this age, however, the dog must be present for the symbolism to work.
- 13-18 months: The child builds a large receptive (or listening) vocabulary.

He understands many more words than he speaks.

- 18 months: The child is well on his way to full symbolic thought. Now he can produce and understand words like "doggie" even if the dog is not present. He is beginning to understand cause and effect.
- 19-24 months: Language acquisition explodes. The child starts using short sentences. Expressive (or speaking) vocabulary starts growing at a rapid pace. Overall vocabulary, receptive and expressive, grows at a rate of 7-12 words per day!
- 24 months: In 2 short years, the overall cognitive changes have been monumental. "The child has moved from sensorimotor intelligence to truly symbolic thought."[19] This symbolic intelligence now allows the child, through speech, to communicate with anyone else who shares the common language.

The ability to think symbolically is necessary for speech to develop. That same ability, already in place at age 2, is the main requirement for learning how to read. A symbol is something that "stands for," or "represents," something else. A two-year old fully understands that the *spoken* word, MAN, symbolizes a living, real man. What is to stop that same two-year old from understanding that, if the letter M symbolizes the sound "mmm," the letter A symbolizes the sound "ahhh," and the letter N symbolizes "nnn," then the letter string M-A-N symbolizes the spoken word, MAN, as well as an actual man?

There are other requirements for learning how to read. The child must have the visual acuity to distinguish between small, similar-looking symbols like "b" and "d," and a large enough receptive vocabulary to make learning to read worthwhile. (All those receptive vocabulary words will quickly become expressive in the course of learning to read.) The child must have the desire and the opportunity to learn to read. And finally, the child needs a willing, patient, and knowledgeable teacher.

If your child is not yet two, here are a few other suggestions for preparing him for the reading program in this book. Once the language explosion has begun, at 18 months, deliberately teach him 3 new vocabulary words per week. This simple step will provide him with 150 more known words than he would otherwise have by age 30 months. Once you've decided on the word, use it repeatedly throughout the day and review it the following day. Encourage your child to use it as well. Look through the early appendices in the back of this book for lots of suggestions.

Finally, sing to (and with) your child. It relaxes her, it's pleasurable, and it gets endorphins flowing through her brain. It teaches her patterns, rhythms, and rhymes – and it reinforces the 41 sounds of English in a novel manner. Be sure to include in your repertoire the singing of the alphabet, which has many of the sounds your child will soon have to master. If you want to get a little head start on Stage 1, get (or make) a poster featuring the 26 uppercase letters. As you sing or recite the alphabet, point to the individual letters.

Don't yield to the temptation to sit her down with a TV, tablet, or computer screen. I encourage you to read the Policy Statement of the American Academy of Pediatrics on this issue.[20] Here are that Policy Statement's main points:

- Children younger than 18 months need hands-on exploration and social interaction with trusted caregivers to develop their cognitive, language, and social-emotional skills. No screen media is recommended other than video-chatting with a close relative.
- If parents want to introduce digital media to children 18-24 months old, the media should only be high-quality programming and/or apps. The parent should watch or use the digital media *with* the child and reteach the content of that media. No solo use, on the part of the child, is recommended at this early age.
- Children 2-5 years old can learn words from live video-chatting with a responsive adult or from an interactive touchscreen interface that tailors its response to what the child does. However, time should be limited to no more than 1 hour per day.
- Children 2-5 years old can also benefit from well-designed television programs like *Sesame Street*. Most programs found under the "education" category in app stores have no evidence of efficacy and they target only rote academic skills.
- Early use of media is a significant predictor of cognitive, language, and social-emotional delays.
- Parents' background use of television distracts from parent-child interactions and child play.
- Heavy parent use of smartphones is associated with fewer interactions between parents and children.

These are tough-to-follow guidelines. I am in full agreement, however, with the first one regarding children under 18 months of age. Such a child is trying to make sense of, what is for him, a brand-new world. What are its rules? How does such a young child distinguish between real and virtual worlds? How is he to understand a world where a scene can *instantaneously* change? Why should he pay attention to something that can simply disappear, without warning? All too quickly, an infant or a toddler can be over-stimulated by the sights and sounds of media. In the first two years of life, what he needs more than anything else is your voice and your personal, loving interaction with him. Nothing substitutes for this – and nothing better prepares him for reading.

References:

1. Robert Owens, *Language Development: An Introduction* (Boston: Pearson Publishing, 2005), 125.

2. Jill Stamm, *Bright from the Start* (New York: Penguin Group, 2007), 20.

3. Owens, *Language Development*, 125.

4. Stamm, *Bright from the Start*, 11-13.

5. Myelin is a fatty substance that surrounds a brain cell's finger-like projections called axons. It facilitates the transmission of electric signals across synapses.

6. John Medina, *Brain Rules for Baby: How to Raise a Smart and Happy Child from Zero to Five* (Seattle, Pear Press, 2010), 33.

7. Stamm, *Bright from the Start*, 15.

8. Ibid., 16-20.

9. Ibid., 21-2.

10. Daniel Rigney, *The Matthew Effect: How Advantage Begets Further Advantage* (New York, Columbia University Press, 2010), 25-81.

11. "Adult Literacy in America," 3rd ed., National Center for Educational Statistics, U.S. Department of Education, April 2002, xvi – xviii. <https://nces.ed.gov/pubs93/93275.pdf> (Accessed 14 Feb 2017).

12. "The Nation's Report Card," National Assessment of Educational Progress, 2015. <https://www.nationsreportcard.gov/reading_math_2015/#reading?grade=4> (Accessed 14 Feb 2017).

13. Owens, *Language Development*, 130-31.

14. Stamm, *Bright from the Start*, 208.

15. Owens, *Language Development*, 138.

16. Hence the importance, if the child is to be bilingual, of hearing that second language throughout the first year of life.

17. Stamm, *Bright from the Start*, 218.

18. Owens, *Language Development*, 140-41.

19. Ibid., 141.

20. "Media and Young Minds," American Academy of Pediatrics, October 2016. <http://pediatrics.aappublications.org/content/early/2016/10/19/peds.2016-2591> (Accessed 14 Feb 2017).

Chapter 2
The Nature of Reading and Spelling

A marvelous code underlies all skilled reading and spelling. You and I are using this code right now. I encoded some thoughts onto this page using various alphabetic characters; you're decoding those characters and reconstructing my thoughts. It's as though I were speaking to you directly. For mature writers and readers, this *encoding* and *decoding* is quick and effortless. Because most of us were quite young when we learned to read, we've probably forgotten the multi-year effort that was required to get us to this point. And because reading and writing are so easy for us now, we may take these skills for granted, failing to appreciate how extraordinary it is that we can draw sound on paper and absorb language with our eyes.

By itself, the alphabet is only part of the code. If its letters aren't explicitly linked to individual sounds, the alphabet is simply a group of 26 abstract, meaningless characters. What follows are the first two sentences of this paragraph repeated, using letters that don't symbolize sound for you. (I simply shifted my fingers one key to the right as I retyped these 2 sentences.)

Nu oydrag, yjr saqjsnry od pmau qsty pg yjr vpfr. Og oyd aryyrtd strm'y rcqaovoyau aomlrf yp omfobisa dpimfd, yjr saqjsnry od dozqau s htpiq pg 26 sndytsvy, zrsmomhardd vjstsvyrtd.

This is how all text must have once appeared to you and me, before we learned the sound value of letters. It's how text appears to every beginning reader. It must be intimidating for a child, especially if her reading instructor *starts* with whole words. (While most reading programs in today's elementary schools do start instruction with whole words, this reading program does not.)

There are 26 letters in our alphabet and 41 elemental sounds in spoken English (see Table 1). The code is what specifies how these letters and sounds are connected: how each of the 26 letters symbolize one or more of these 41 elemental sounds, and how each of the 41 sounds can be spelled. Understanding the code is the key to learning *both* spelling and reading because these 2 skills are the opposite of one another. To spell (or write), one encodes sound onto paper using various alphabetic symbols. To read, one decodes those written symbols back into sound. Armed with the alphabet, and knowledge of the code that animates it, we can depict the million words of English on paper, using only 26 symbols.

Phonics is the study of this code for the express purpose of learning to read and spell. Without phonics, the alphabet is simply a collection of strange characters, but with it, the alphabet is a powerful tool for recording sound on paper – even the sound of our private thoughts. By teaching your child to read phonetically, you'll make reading and spelling *logical* for her. Once she discovers this logic it will fascinate and delight her. Seeing that reading and spelling are based on reason (rather than on rote memorization of "sight words"), she'll be motivated to make the year-long effort required to master these two critical skills. By using this book's 18-stage program to teach your child how to read and spell, you'll be using phonics from start to finish – and your child will become a confident, skilled reader and a capable speller.

I do *not* mean to imply you must master phonics (the full code) before you start teaching your child. On the contrary, unless you're a linguist, I expect you'll be learning (or re-learning) phonics right along with your child as this program progresses. I'll be guiding you through each step – so don't be concerned that you don't already know everything that will be necessary. You'll learn (and then teach) as you go. A summary of the full code, from opposite perspectives, can be found in this book in appendices P and Q.

That said, there is one item I hope you *will* learn before starting this program. That item is the special notation involving slash marks, / /, which you can find throughout Table 1. I'll make you two promises. First, it won't take you long to get comfortable with this notation, and second, you won't have to teach it to your child. The notation is only to facilitate accurate communication between you and me. (I'll be discussing Table 1 for the remainder of this chapter, so you may want to bookmark it.)

Every word you've ever spoken (in English) consists of one or more of the 41 sounds listed in Table 1. As I indicate there, 17 are vowel sounds and 24 are consonant sounds. They are the unique building blocks of our spoken, common language. Think of them as the equivalent of the 118 chemical elements or atoms in the Periodic Table. Just as those atoms form the basis of all the matter in our physical world, the 41 sounds in Table 1 form the basis of all the words we'll ever speak. (The analogy is not perfect because, under extraordinary conditions, atoms can be split; these 41 sounds, however, are un-split-able!)

So why do we need a special notation to deal with these 41 unique sounds? After all, when teaching them to your child you'll *always* speak them. So why the notation? Here's the problem. Suppose I want to discuss the short O sound with you. That's the first sound you can hear in the word OX or ODD. Since I'm not physically present to you, I can't speak it. I could try to spell the sound for you, OH perhaps, but OH is commonly viewed as the spelling for *long* O, as in "Uh-oh! I dropped your priceless vase!" or "Oh my! There's a fly in my tomato soup!" Maybe I could spell the short O sound using AH, as when a doctor says, "Open your mouth and say ah." But then how would I spell the short A sound (the first sound in the word APPLE)? Further, how would I spell the sound of a consonant like D: DEH? DAH? DUH?

I think you can see that spelling these elemental sounds would lead to confusion. On the other hand, the notation I use in Table 1 is precise. Right next to each sound are 2 or 3 words using the sound. When I refer to /oo/, for example, later in this book – and if you've temporarily forgotten how it sounds – you can quickly look it up in Table 1 where you'll see it occurs in the words GOOD, BOOK, and WOOL. In most cases, the letter(s) between the slash marks will remind you how to pronounce the sound. For instance, /ew/ is pronounced like the word NEW, but without the N. (Throughout this entire 18-stage program, whenever you see something surrounded by slash marks, I strongly encourage you to *speak it aloud* rather than read it silently.)

Here are some examples to help you get accustomed to the notation. As you examine Table 1, you'll probably notice I designate short vowels sounds with lowercase letters (/a/ /e/ /o/) and long vowel sounds with uppercase (/A/ /E/ /O/). With that in mind, look at these two statements:

HAT = /h/ + /a/ + /t/
HATE = /h/ + /A/ + /t/

On the left are the *spellings* of two common English words; on the right are the exact 3 *sounds* you can hear in each of these words. Simply blend the 3 sounds together, quickly and smoothly, and you'll produce the word. The E in HATE is only a spelling convention (covered in Stage 11 in this reading program) and, as such, it has no sound. Here's another example:

WAG = /w/ + /a/ + /g/
WAGE = /w/ + /A/ + /j/

Again, the spelling is on the left while the actual sounds present in the word are on the right. The notation again makes clear these two words have different vowel sounds. In addition, it makes clear that, although both words are spelled with a G, the second word ends in a J sound rather than a G sound. GE is a common spelling convention for the sound of J (see Stage 17).

English spelling can sometimes be confusing, partly because there are so many homophones (words that sound the same but have different spellings and meanings):

WAIST = WASTE = /w/ + /A/ + /s/ + /t/
TO = TOO = TWO = /t/ + /ew/

And, of course, there are a few English spellings that make no sense whatsoever, given the actual sounds present in the word's pronunciation:

ONE = /w/ + /u/ + /n/
OF = /u/ + /v/

Spelling is necessarily complex in English for a simple reason: our language has more elemental sounds (41) than it has letters (26) to symbolize them. This results in a more complex code than is found in other alphabetic languages like Italian and German. In the above HAT/HATE example, you saw how the single letter A can symbolize 2 different sounds: /a/ and /A/. The opposite is also true. A single sound can be spelled in more than one way:

ZOO = /z/ + /ew/
NEW = /n/ + /ew/
BLUE = /b/ + /l/ + /ew/
FRUIT = /f/ + /r/ + /ew/ + /t/

This example shows the sound /ew/ can be spelled OO, EW, UE, and UI.

Though this final example is a little trickier, it shows a number of phonics topics that will be covered in the reading program later in this book. Let's take the two words, PHONICS and CITY, and using this new notation, again state the precise sounds that can be heard in each of them. Try to do this yourself before reading any further. (Hint: there is no /c/ among the 41 sounds of English.)

PHONICS = /f/ + /o/ + /n/ + /i/ + /k/ + /s/
CITY = /s/ + /i/ + /t/ + /E/

Three important phonics topics are illustrated here. First, the sound /f/ is sometimes spelled PH rather than F. Second, the letter C always spells either the sound /k/ or /s/. Finally, the letter Y can act as a vowel. When it does, it usually spells long E.

Note: If the notation across from CITY (above) looks like the word SITE to you, it's because you are confusing spelling with sound. The slash mark notation has nothing to do with spelling; it simply specifies sound. Here are 11 similar-sounding words that differ from each other *only* in their vowel sound(s):

SIT = /s/ + /i/ + /t/
SITE = /s/ + /I/ + /t/
SET = /s/ + /e/ + /t/
SEAT = /s/ + /E/ + /t/
SAT = /s/ + /a/ + /t/
SATE = /s/ + /A/ + /t/
SUIT = /s/ + /ew/ + /t/
SOT = /s/ + /o/ + /t/
SOOT = /s/ + /oo/ + /t/
SOUGHT = /s/ + /aw/ + /t/
CITY = /s/ + /i/ + /t/ + /E/

My only goal in the above examples was to get you more accustomed to my slash mark notation for sounds. Everything else will be gradually presented to you (and thus to your child) during the course of this program's 18 stages.

One more thing: if you looked through Table 1 carefully, you may be wondering why /c/, /q/, /x/, and /U/ are missing. You may also be puzzling over those two uppercase versions of /th/ and /sh/. While these apparent omissions and additions will be fully explained in the course of this program, here is a quick preview:

- There is no unique sound /c/ because the *letter* C itself is unnecessary. CAT could be spelled KAT. CITY could be spelled SITY (as it is in UNIVERSITY). Since the sounds /k/ and /s/ are already listed in Table 1, including /c/ would add no new sound.
- I omit /q/ for the same reason. Every word spelled with QU could instead be spelled with KW (compare QUACK and KWACK). Since /k/ and /w/ are already on the list, /q/ is unnecessary.
- The same reasoning holds for /x/. Every word ending in X could instead be spelled with KS (compare BOX and BOKS). Since /k/ and /s/ are already on the list, we don't need the sound /x/.
- The sound /U/ (long U) can easily be produced by sounds already on the list: /U/ = /y/ + /ew/.
- The /th/ sound (lowercase) is a sound made with *air only*. You can hear it in the words THIN, THICK, and MOTH. The /TH/ sound (uppercase) is a similar sound, but it's made with the *vocal cords*. You can hear it in the words THIS, THAT, and MOTHER. Try it yourself! /TH/ is voiced; /th/ is

voiceless.

- Similarly, /sh/ is voiceless. You can hear it in SHIP, CASH, and MISSION. /SH/ is voiced. You can hear it in the words VISION, PLEASURE, and ASIA, even though these words are not spelled with the letters SH.

This voiced/voiceless distinction occurs for many letter pairs in English, as you can see (or hear) in this table:

Voiced	Unvoiced
/TH/	/th/
/SH/	/sh/
/b/	/p/
/d/	/t/
/g/	/k/
/j/	/ch/
/z/	/s/
/v/	/f/

Notice for each of these pairs, the mouth and tongue are in the same configuration – the only difference is voicing versus air alone. Happily, in most cases, English uses a different letter for the voiced and unvoiced version of a given sound. It is only in the case of /th/ and /sh/ that English does not have a unique spelling for the voiced and voiceless versions of the sound.

Note: Some linguists include /wh/ as a unique sound, separate from /w/. They claim the sound /wh/ is what you hear if someone pronounces the word WHEN as HWEN. Now it may be that some people pronounce WHEN in this manner. Hwether or not this is true, however, I think it's too subtle for the beginning reader and is therefore an unnecessary distraction. You can teach your child that, for the letter combination WH, the H is silent. In other words, he'll pronounce the word WHEN as WEN.

Don't stress over this notation. Once you can look through the list of the 41 elemental sounds in Table 1 and, out loud, correctly pronounce all (or most) of them, you are ready to move on to Chapter 3. Table 1 is always there for reference if you need it later on. When working with your child, the two of you will always speak these sounds; he'll never see this written, specialized notation.

Chapter 3
Systematic Phonics

Y ou should be aware that phonics is not the only method for teaching a child to read. Since 1920 or so, there has been another widely-used method for teaching literacy. It's called Whole Word. During the middle of the previous century, Whole Word was known as the Look/Say method. During the 80s and 90s, it was called Whole Language. Now it's known as Balanced Literacy or The Balanced Approach. Systematic Phonics and Whole Word are not compatible.

Using Systematic Phonics, a teacher starts with letters and the sounds those letters symbolize, and then she carefully shows the child how to blend those sounds into words. Unfamiliar words are decoded, that is, "sounded out" based on their constituent letters. Systematic Phonics is a *bottom-up* approach to reading where the child learns the entire code in a carefully sequenced and systematic manner.

Using the Whole Word method, a teacher starts, as the name suggests, with whole words. Since these words can't be read by the beginner, they must be memorized as "sight words." When a child encounters an unfamiliar word (a word not previously memorized as a sight word), she is encouraged to guess its meaning. The guessing is based on the word's context within the sentence, or on a picture accompanying the text, or on the word's first letter. Whole Word is a *top-down* approach to reading that either ignores the code, or teaches a small part of it as an aid to the word-guessing that is intrinsic to its methodology.

Whole Word methods have been dominant in the nation's schools since 1920 despite disastrous results on national reading tests[1] and despite the conclusions of the National Reading Panel. That Panel was convened by the U.S. Congress in 1997 with the mandate to examine all available scientific research on how to teach children to read, and to determine the most effective method. In its 480-page final report in 2000, the Panel concluded Systematic Phonics, not Whole Word, was the best method for teaching both reading and spelling.[2]

The National Reading Panel used the adjective "systematic" to describe the phonics it was endorsing for good reason: there were (and are) numerous versions of phonics that are not at all systematic. They go by such names as "analytic" phonics, "embedded" phonics, "analogy" phonics, and "onset-and-rime" phonics. What's common to all these non-systematic versions of phonics is they teach only a small part of the code. In addition, they're not methods for teaching literacy; they're simply phonetic aids to help a student with the word-guessing that's at the heart of the Whole Word method.

When I taught reading to my three preschool children nearly two decades ago, using phonics, I was unaware Whole Word was being used in most of the local schools. It was clear to me then – and it's clear to me now – that if we want to teach a child to read an *alphabetic* language (as opposed to Mandarin or Japanese), and if we want to respect that child's need to understand *why* words are spelled as they are, we should teach the full code. You can take my word for the superiority of Systematic Phonics, or you can take the National Reading Panel's word, or, best of all, you can simply trust your own common sense. In any case, the reading method you are about to use with your child is full-code, authentic, Systematic Phonics (hereafter referred to, simply, as "phonics").

Phonics

Phonics is not a tool to help a student with word-guessing in a Whole Word reading program. Instead, it's a singularly effective *method* for teaching both reading and spelling. As you use the program in this book, you'll find phonics has *all* the following characteristics:

- The code is taught *explicitly* (because most children can't discover how it works on their own).
- The *entire* code is taught, not only parts of it.
- Instruction begins with individual letters and the sounds those letters symbolize. It does not start with whole words.
- The skill of *blending* individual sounds into whole words is explicitly modeled and taught.
- Instruction is *systematic.* The code is presented in a carefully sequenced and logical manner with each new topic building on what the child has already mastered.
- Memorization of sight words is kept to an absolute minimum. (In this program, you'll teach only 5 such words.)
- The child is taught to handle an unknown word by decoding it rather than using context or pictures to guess what it might be.
- The child is asked to read only *decodable* text, that is, text for which he already has the skills needed to succeed.

Genuine phonics programs can differ from each other, not in the above characteristics, but in some other, less essential areas. These include: the order in which the teacher presents the full code, how early blending (and therefore reading) is introduced, how and when spelling comes into play, how to handle irregular words, what notation to use, how many rules to feature, and whether to reserve significant daily time for reading *to* the child. How I handle these less essential areas is detailed below, and, of course, in the 18-stage reading program itself.

Rules

A primary goal in this program is to get your child to independent reading *as quickly as possible.* In pursuit of this goal, we'll keep the vocabulary, the rules, and the sight words your child must memorize to an absolute minimum. For example, while your child *will* need to know the meaning of "vowel" and "consonant," she'll not need to learn any specialized notation and she'll not be required to memorize more than a few sight words.

This version of phonics gives special attention to 14 common letter combinations that are not phonetic, that is, their actual pronunciations are at odds with their spellings. I list them at the end of Appendix Q. Knowing them, however, makes thousands of additional words perfectly phonetic. You'll explore all 14 of these letter strings with your child at various stages in this reading program. Here is an example of one of them: both TION and SION are pronounced "SHIN." With this simple rule, ACTION, MISSION, TENSION, and hundreds of similar words become "phonetic."

Irregular Words

English has more spelling irregularities than most other alphabetic languages. These irregularities complicate the task of teaching someone to read. I estimate, however, that 95% of the words a student will see and use through high school are perfectly regular, based on the phonics I present in this program. That still leaves quite a few irregular words. I studied various lists featuring the 500 most-used words in the English language (easy to find online) and picked out the words that might still be considered irregular, even after having mastered *all* the phonics in this program. I found 50 such words and listed them in Appendix S. If you look at that list, the Tricky 50, you'll see I also provide a spelling that would make these words regular.

When these 50 tricky words start showing up, in Stage 9 of this program, you'll simply call your child's attention to them. You'll focus, not on the word's irregularities, but on what is *regular* about them. For example, HAVE, ARE, WERE, and GIVE are perfectly regular if we simply drop the final E. Other tricky words are regular in both their first and last letter (COULD, WANT, FRIEND). You'll sometimes ask your child how the tricky word would be spelled if we lived in a perfectly phonetic world. For instance, SAID would be spelled SED in such a world.

The only thing you *won't* do is have your child memorize these 50 words as sight words – unless it's unavoidable. It becomes unavoidable when a word is spelled so wildly, given its sounds, there is no choice but to simply memorize it. I count only five such words on the Tricky 50 list: EYE, ONE, ONCE, EIGHT, and OF (I, WUN, WUNS, ATE, UV). (As promised, this phonics program will keep memorization of sight words to a minimum!)

What happens when a young reader comes across the occasional irregular word *not* included among the Tricky 50? Similarly, what happens when she meets a homograph like WIND – a word which has two correct pronunciations and two different meanings? (WIND can be the noun you experience in a storm or the verb you do to a clock). In such cases, she'll improvise. She'll make an educated guess based, first, on her phonics skills, and then on the context of the word. She'll learn from experience doing actual reading. Further, she is unlikely to encounter many such exceptions during her first year or two of independent reading, because her focus will be on material written primarily for younger children.

An Illusion

I've structured this phonics program in such a way that for the first 6 stages, you'll be able to teach reading as though English is a perfectly phonetic language: one with no spelling irregularities or exceptions. You'll act as though each letter in the alphabet has a single sound, and each sound is symbolized by a single letter. You'll be able to sustain this illusion until midway through Stage 7, when Q, X, and "silent" letters first appear.

I've done this because, in the earliest stages, I want your child to become firmly convinced reading is easy and logical – and therefore worth the effort. You won't present your child with any "complications" until well after she has concluded "Reading is fun," "Reading makes sense," and "By darn, I can do it!" Only when these critically important convictions are firmly entrenched in her mind will you *slowly* start to reveal the "anomalies" of English. By then, these anomalies will cause her little concern or confusion because she'll be confident in her reading ability and because she'll understand the overwhelming logic of the code.

Motivation

Some long-running complaints of phonics are that it's boring, that it involves tedious drill work, and that a child will lose interest in it long before he ever gets to read a simple poem or story. I suppose this *could* be true if reading was needlessly delayed, if the instruction was unimaginative and humorless, and if the teacher used the entire class time for nothing but repetitive drill work. That will not be the case here. Powerful motivation in this phonics program will derive primarily from three factors:

1) Reading starts early. It's not delayed until the middle or end of the program, rather, it starts right at the beginning, in Stage 2. There, with only 8 (of the 41) elemental sounds mastered, your child, with your help, will start blending those sounds into words like MOM, MAN, and SUN. And when I say "reading," I mean *decoding* the words, not memorizing them as sight words. Based on my experience teaching preschoolers, I can confirm that, once authentic reading begins, motivation is not an issue. A child becomes proud and enthusiastic – perceiving herself as starting to master the skill all the significant adults in her life can do.

2) Your child begins to understand the *logic* that underlies the skill of reading. She starts to glimpse what linguists call the Alphabetic Principle: written words are distinguishable from one another, not by their overall shape or by their individual letters, but by the sounds those individual letters symbolize. She begins to appreciate print is simply coded sound, and that insight makes her eager to learn more about the code.

3) In this program, and in any phonics program worth mentioning, you'll spend time each day not only teaching phonics, but also reading classic children's literature *to* your child. You'll read to him daily, not that he might acquire a few sight words, but that he'll become enchanted by the stories you tell. You won't simply read, you'll facilitate a discussion: "Why do you think Jack did that?" "What do you think the giant will do next?" Listening to quality literature provides enormous motivation for a phonics student. He'll want to continue his phonics lessons because he wishes, one day soon, to read such stories on his own, and not simply listen.

Becoming Aware of Sound

Illiterate people, both children and adults, are usually unaware of the 41 elemental sounds of English I've listed in Table 1. That's because in speech, these individual sounds are *coarticulated*, that is, they seamlessly blend into one another. Neither the speaker, nor the listener, need be aware of them because the brain's language center handles these coarticulated sounds automatically and unconsciously. However, for skilled *reading* and *spelling* to occur, these 41 elemental sounds must be brought into full, conscious awareness. The phonics program you are about to use does this explicitly and systematically. It *must* do so because phonics depends upon the reader's ability to match letters with the sounds they symbolize. Such matching can't occur until the reader becomes consciously aware of these 41 sounds. You'll start bringing these sounds to your child's attention in Stage 2 when you teach her "A says /a/." (Remember: when you see something surrounded by slash marks, speak it aloud rather than read it silently.)

The main point I want to make about sound-awareness is that phonics *starts* with the 41 elemental sounds, and then teaches the new reader how to blend them into words. Your child can't possibly avoid becoming aware of these sounds. You'll be training her to hear them – and to match them with appropriate letters – throughout this entire program. As the National Reading Panel concluded in its final report, this basic sound-awareness will have a strong positive impact, not only on her reading, but on her spelling as well.

Spelling

A competent speller is one who can hear the elemental sounds in a spoken word (sound-awareness) and then match each of those sounds with an appropriate letter (or letters). For a phonics student, hearing those sounds is relatively easy. That's because each word he can read he has previously built from the ground up. For him, each word begins as a collection of *individual* sounds. He then blends those sounds into a whole word. Naturally, if he first assembles a word in this manner, he'll find it easier, upon hearing the word, to take it apart, sound by sound, match those sounds with appropriate letters, and thereby spell it. In this program, spelling begins in Stage 4.

*   *   *   *   *

I hope you'll take the time to read through the entire 18-stage program before starting to teach. Doing so will answer many questions you may now have, and it will provide you with a broad overview of what constitutes a genuine phonics program. At a minimum, read each individual stage completely before starting it with your child. I tend to intersperse discussion meant for you alone, with suggestions for how to approach your child. Doing an initial read of the entire stage should help to clarify which is which. In all cases, anything surrounded with slash marks is meant to be spoken aloud, not read silently.

References:

1. On the most recent national test of 8th grade reading skills, 2 out of 3 students were judged deficient in their reading ability. See "The Nation's Report Card," National Assessment of Educational Progress, 2015. <https://www.nationsreportcard.gov/reading_math_2015/#reading?grade=4> (Accessed 14 Feb 2017).
2. The Full Report of the National Reading Panel, *Teaching Children to Read*, can be found at https://www.nichd.nih.gov/publications/pubs/nrp/documents/report.pdf (Accessed 8 July 2017).

A Systematic Phonics Program

for

Teaching Literacy

Stage 1
Letter and Number Recognition

Begin the reading program here if your child can't yet recognize all the letters of the alphabet and the ten numerical symbols of our counting system. If your child can recognize *only* uppercase letters, or *only* lowercase letters, you too should begin here. But if she has already mastered the 52 upper and lowercase letters, and can match them, "A" with "a", "B" with "b", and so on, you can proceed to Stage 2. There you'll begin teaching her the sounds that letters symbolize.

Let's discuss goals for Stage 1 and look at some suggestions for arriving at that destination. Your child must be able to name all 52 letters of the alphabet, even when the letters are shown in random order. In addition, he needs to be able to name the first ten digits in our counting system. This totals *62* symbols he needs to know by sight, without any hesitation. We also want him to be able to correctly *order* these symbols, from A to Z, a to z, and 0 to 9 – and we want him to be able to pair up every uppercase letter with its lowercase counterpart. This is especially important for those instances when the two letters do not look alike, for example, G and g, or D and d. It's preferable not to use terminology like "uppercase" and "lowercase" with your child – just say "big A" and "little a" to keep things simple.

To accomplish these goals, the two of you can simply do enjoyable letter and number activities on a daily basis. You've got lots of time for this stage, 6 months if necessary, so don't feel like you need to rush. Naturally, while in Stage 1, you'll continue with the activities discussed in Chapter 1: speaking, singing, and reading to him, as well as deliberately teaching him new vocabulary. What follows are some individual activities and projects that may serve you well during this preliminary stage.

It will help your child's learning if he can hold and manipulate the letters, and arrange them on the floor. The letters can be plastic, foam, or wood, and they can lay flat, stand on their own, or stick to a magnetic surface. They can be the classic wooden cubes that have a letter or a picture painted on each of the 6 sides. Whatever route you choose, get a set large enough so your child can lay out the entire alphabet at one time. Doing a search on Amazon, I found many possibilities from (among other companies) Uncle Goose, Imaginarium, Melissa & Doug, Alex Toys, Lakeshore, Schylling, Hape, We Sell Mats, Maxim, Roscoe, Magtimes, and Pixel Premium.

As an alternative to buying something, you can create your own letters.

Get a stack of 4x6 index cards and some colorful, broad-tipped magic markers. Cut each card in three equal parts, resulting in a pile of 2x4 cards. Then, using a pencil, lightly divide each 2x4 card into three equal zones as illustrated. From top to bottom, I'll call them zones 1, 2, and 3.

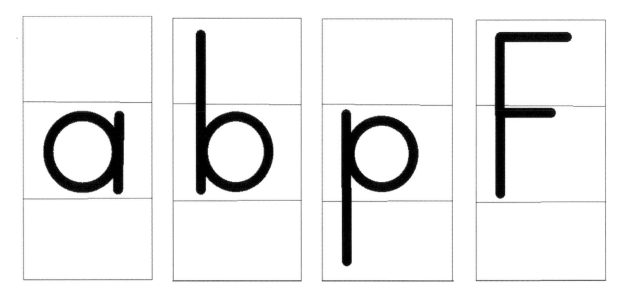

Now, using the magic markers, draw a letter on each card, using only zone 2 for lowercase letters without stems (a, c, e, m and so on). Those with stems can be drawn in zones 1 and 2 (b, d, k) or in zones 2 and 3 (p, q, g). All the uppercase letters can be drawn in zones 1 and 2. Alternate the colors if you like. Now you have a 52-card deck of both upper and lowercase letters your child can manipulate. You can also create a deck of number cards as well. Conveniently, all these cards are easy to replace if one gets lost or damaged.

Now, when your child sings the alphabet, she can lay out the letters on the floor, surrounding herself as she places them in order. I would focus on uppercase letters first; they are a little easier for a child to draw and to recognize. Initially, help as much as she needs and then let her arrange the letters herself as she gets better. Gradually call her attention to the slight differences between similarly constructed letters like the circle-and-stem group (b, d, p, q, and a) or the hump-and-stem group (h, u, n, and m). Point out the similarities between the letters E and F, A and V, T and I, O and Q, C and G, P and B. For more memory-reinforcing games, ask her to make 3 piles of letters: those using only straight lines, those using only curves, and those using both lines and curves. You can also ask her to separate the upper and lowercase letter pairs into two piles: one where the child looks like the parent (P, p) and the other where the child does not (A, a).

Note: For the fonts used in most books, lowercase A and G look like this:

a g

However, most children, at least initially, learn to recognize these letters when they are drawn this way:

a g

There is no way around this problem, so deal with it directly. Point it out and discuss it with your child. He needs to recognize both versions of these letters.

There are many other activities the two of you can do together to help him learn his letters. Get, or borrow, alphabet books for your daily reading sessions. Some particularly helpful ones are:

- *ABC* (Dr. Seuss)
- *Alphabet Under Construction* (Fleming)
- *Alpha Oops: The Day Z Went First* (Kontis)
- *The Alphabet Tree* (Lionni)
- *The Construction Alphabet Book* (Pallotta)
- *The Alphabet Book* (Eastman)
- *Eating the Alphabet* (Ehlert)
- *Numbers Colors Shapes* (Priddy)
- *ABC* (Carle)
- *Alphablock* (Franceschelli)
- *Alphabet Adventure* (Wood)
- *Chicka Chicka Boom Boom* (Martin)
- *Best Word Book Ever* (Scarry)

As you read to him, start pointing out that sentences always start with a big letter and end with a period. In using these books, you are interested in letter recognition only; avoid encouraging him to memorize whole words.

If you are dealing with an older child whose motor skills allow it, encourage him to write the letters and numbers on paper. With a younger child, you can set the font of a word processor to the largest size available and let him try to type the letters, in order, on a screen. Comic Sans font works well for this activity because the letters look hand-drawn: A a, B b, G g.

There are some free (or at least inexpensive) worthwhile apps your child can use on a smartphone or tablet that can help with letter recognition. Do a search on "alphabet" or "alphabet tracing" and you'll find hundreds of them. The most useful apps for the goals of this stage are those that have the child trace the letters and numbers on a touch screen. I rejected most of the 50 I tested because they committed one or more of the following offenses:

- Obtrusive, full-screen pop-up ads that could not be eliminated.
- Tracing that is unforgiving (too picky) and is therefore likely to frustrate the child.
- Associating unhelpful words with letters, such as "chicken" with C, "ship" with S, and "orange" with O. These words may start with the correct letter, but they have a misleading initial sound.
- Associating unhelpful sounds with letters, such as "buh" for B. "Buh" is a helpful sound for B if you're trying to read BUS; it's unhelpful if you're trying to read BIG, BAG, BED, or BOG.

In general, avoid apps whose primary focus is sound. The goal, for now, is letter recognition only. Here are 5 apps I found useful and well-structured: *Writing Wizard, Interactive Alphabet, Alive Alphabet Letter Tracing, ABC 123 Writing Coloring Book,* and *123s ABCs Handwriting Fun.* If you choose to use some apps during this stage, recall the guidelines from the American Academy of Pediatrics, discussed earlier in Chapter 1. According to those guidelines, up to an hour per day of supervised time with high-quality programming or apps, is appropriate for the 2-5 age group.

Purchase (or make) a large, colorful alphabet/number poster for the wall, hung low enough so your child can reach it. Ask him to point to various letters or numbers you specify, and then reverse roles and allow him to quiz you. (Deliberately make some mistakes so he gets the pleasure of correcting you.)

Count things with him wherever you go. Have him use his fingers to show he understands the meanings of the numbers 1 through 10. It won't be long before he's counting independently. If he is old enough to use a crayon or a pencil, have him draw 2 stars or 3 circles or 4 triangles or 6 rectangles and so on, teaching shapes as well as quantities. If he shows the slightest interest, show him what comes after 10. He can show his age on his fingers. You can show him *your* age by writing down all the numbers needed to count from 1 to whatever that figure might be.

Every time you go for a walk, encourage your child to "read" car license plates. These plates typically mix uppercase letters with numbers. Children love to recite these letters and numbers when walking or riding in a stroller. This activity can't be done at the start of Stage 1, but as your child makes progress, she'll begin to enjoy this challenge. Also, if you're doing shapes, point out the octagons (stop signs) on your walk and have her count the number of sides in this common shape. Do the same for signs shaped like rectangles, circles, or triangles.

With only 12 different shapes, your child can "build" each upper and lowercase letter side by side. For this more ambitious project, you'll need some real or homemade clay. To find the real stuff, google "Sculpey Clay" or "Crayola Clay" on Amazon. The Sculpey clay needs oven-drying for your shapes to cure and harden; the Crayola version will air dry. For homemade versions of "clay," google it and you'll find multiple sites and recipes. Some use salt and flour, others use baking soda and cornstarch. For under 10 dollars, the real clay works better than the homemade (because it's more durable) but both will do the job.

The 12 shapes and their sizes are shown below. You'll need to make 3 of each stem and 2 of everything else (except for the small S – you need only one of that shape). Thus, the 12 pictured shapes become 27 individual pieces. For the 2 semi-circles, start with stems 6 and 13 cm long and then curve them into the size indicated on the drawing. For the 2 J's, start with stems 8 and 10 cm long; for the two C's, 10 and 20 cm long. The small R starts out at 6 cm while the small S starts at 8 cm. Each piece should be about the width of a pencil.

I chose these quantities and shapes so an upper and lowercase version of any letter can be built *at the same time*. All uppercase letters will be 8 cm high. Lowercase letters without stems (a, e, u) will be 4 cm high; those with stems will be 6 or 8 cm high, depending on the length of the stem chosen. I suggest giving your child a blank piece of paper with a single line drawn on it so she can practice correct placement of the letters she builds. (Some letters must extend below the line.) There's nothing like piecing something together in order to remember its shape forever!

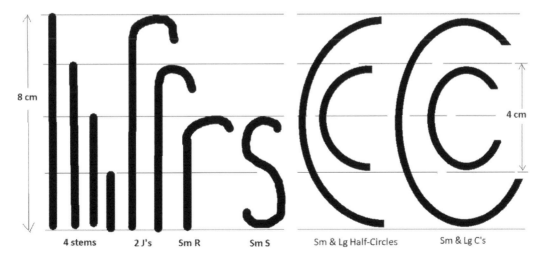

| 4 stems | 2 J's | Sm R | Sm S | Sm & Lg Half-Circles | Sm & Lg C's |

If you don't immediately see how these shapes can be formed into any upper or lowercase letter, some clarifications might help. The small R shape in the above drawing, besides being used for small R, is also used in the construction of small H, M, N, and U. Large S can be made from the semi-circles. The small C is used for small A, B, D, E, G, P, and Q as well. Either J can also be used as the stem for small G. If you prefer complete O's without piecing them together from the semi-circles, use a piece of clay 24 cm long for the large O and 12 cm long for the small. For dotting the small I and the small J, use Cheerios or peas.

You may have other ideas as well; use whatever works to help your child learn to identify his letters and numbers. You'll be done with Stage 1 when he can pass the following test. With the 52 letter symbols and 10 number symbols mixed up together in a pile on the floor, see if he can line them up:

A, a, B, b, C, c, ... Z, z   and   0, 1, 2, ...9

If he can do this quickly and efficiently, without mistakes, he's ready to move on. By the end of Stage 2, he'll be reading.

Teacher Note: In many ways, Stage 1 is preliminary to this reading program. A beginner must be able to distinguish the letters before he can learn what sound each letter symbolizes. Stages 2-18 constitute the core program. You'll notice I don't include any guidelines for how much time to devote to each of the forthcoming stages. But keep this in mind: Stages 2-18 are going to take about a year. For some kids, it may be only 8 months; for others, a year-and-a-half.

Let's assume a year. That's 52 weeks divided by 17 stages – or roughly 3 weeks per stage. But here's the problem with such a tidy calculation. The stages are not of equal length or difficulty. Some stages may go faster than 3 weeks; others will certainly go slower. My advice is not to concern yourself with time. Stay with the topics in a given stage until you are convinced your child has mastered what is presented there.

Topics within stages are divided by horizontal lines. These lines simply signal the next topic. They do not mean all the material between horizontal lines should be done in a single lesson. They are simply logical breaks.

Stage 2
The Sounds of A, E, I, O, U, M, N, S
Reading Begins

Y ou're ready to begin this stage of the reading program if your child has mastered the letter and number recognition skills from Stage 1. (This stage could be your starting point if you will be teaching an older child.) From this point on, however, doing all stages in order is a necessity for anyone who wishes to teach reading phonetically. Stages 2 through 7 form a foundation for everything that follows. In these initial stages, you'll teach individual letter sounds, as well as the critical skill of blending.

> **Teacher Note**: For this and the following stages, you'll need a large stack of blank 3 x 5 index cards and a few magic markers.

I would like to re-emphasize here what I said in Chapter 3. In these initial stages, you'll be presenting an illusion for your child: that English reading and spelling are regular. In other words, you'll be acting as though each letter in the alphabet symbolizes a single sound, and each sound is spelled by a single letter. You want the learner, especially if the learner is a young child, to conclude that reading is a logical, rational skill – like any skill worth pursuing. Only after he has started reading with some competence and confidence will you gradually start showing him that English has some spelling (and therefore reading) irregularities. In Stages 2 through 7, everything you teach him will be reasonable, logical, and without exceptions.

I also would like to remind you that daily reading to your child is an important motivational part of this program. I recommend the two of you devote about an hour a day to reading lessons: 30-40 minutes devoted to phonics, and 20-30 minutes reserved for reading to him from any quality child's book. Phonics can sometimes be challenging and it often requires significant concentration. On the other hand, the time he spends listening to your enchanting stories is undiluted fun and relaxation for him. You're the best judge of your child's attention span, his desires, and his capabilities. Whatever time investment you decide on, be sure to supplement the phonics instruction with your reading of children's literature.

First, let's deal with some preliminaries you, as the teacher, need to understand now, and your child will need to understand a little later. All the vowels – A, E, I, O, and U – symbolize *two* primary sounds: one "short" and the other "long." (If necessary, review the list of all 41 elemental sounds in Table 1.)

The other letters of the alphabet, called consonants, have a single primary sound. Of course, that's not entirely accurate. For example, G can have a J sound (GENIUS), C can have an S sound (CITY), and S can have a Z sound (HIS). But these are nuances you'll deal with later. For now, until midway through Stage 7, you'll be acting as though each of the 26 letters of the alphabet symbolizes a *single sound*. This means the five vowels will have only their short sound. Long vowel sounds will appear in later stages.

As the teacher, you need to be clear in your own mind precisely what these five short vowel sounds are before you can teach them to someone else. The consonant sounds are straightforward, but the short vowel sounds can be tricky to master, for you and for your child. (Don't refer to these sounds as "short" with your child. As far as she is concerned, the vowels have only one sound at this point in the program.) Let's look at these short vowel sounds first. You can hear each of their sounds at the start of the following short words:

Vowel	Example	Sound
A	at	/a/
E	egg	/e/
I	in	/i/
O	ox	/o/
U	up	/u/

To firmly lock these five vowel sounds in your memory, practice saying them with a CK attached: ACK, ECK, ICK, OCK, UCK. Then begin saying them *without* the CK attached: /a/, /e/, /i/, /o/, /u/.

These 5 vowel sounds, isolated from any others, are critically important in this and the next 6 stages. As you practice saying these vowel sounds to yourself, notice the shape of your mouth. You'll find the sounds /a/ and /o/ both require a fully-opened mouth. The sound /e/ requires a half-open mouth; both /i/ and /u/ require the mouth to be open only slightly. Once you have these 5 sounds mastered (can you do them backwards? in any order?), you'll be ready to begin this stage with your child. As you do, remember that the slash notation is not for him – he need only produce the correct sound, verbally, when you ask him for it.

In this stage, you'll initially teach your child the sound of 8 letters: A, E, I, O, U, M, N, and S. Why these 8 letters to start? The 5 vowel sounds must be learned at the outset because there is a vowel in every syllable of every word. I picked the consonants M, N, and S because their sounds, /m/, /n/, and /s/, are *sustainable*, like the sounds of the 5 vowels. Your child can make the sounds of each of these 8 letters for as long as he pleases, until his breath gives out. This will make teaching the skill of blending much easier. As soon as your child has mastered these 8 sustainable sounds, you'll teach him how to blend those sounds into familiar words such as MAN, SUN, MESS, SAM, US, and IN. In other words, he'll start reading!

Blending non-sustainable sounds is a little trickier; you'll delay doing that until Stage 3. Examples of sounds that are not sustainable are the sounds of the letters B, D, G, J, K, P, and T.

―――

OK, time to start working with your child. The first goal is to teach him the 5 vowel sounds you just taught yourself. How might you go about doing this? Initially, simply tell him:

"A says /a/"

(Don't show him anything written – simply tell him what A says. You might try this: Dogs say "woof," cats say "meow," A says /a/.) Now ask him:

"Do you know a fruit that starts with the sound /a/?"

If he comes up with the word, fine. If not, tell him:

"Apple begins with /a/" (exaggerate the A sound)

Ask him if he can hear that same A sound, /a/, at the beginning of these words: ALLIGATOR, ACT, ANT, ASK, AFTER, AX, ASHES, ATLAS, ATTIC, ANIMAL, ADD, ANTLERS, ACTION, AFRICA, ALLEY, AMBULANCE, ALPHABET, ASTEROID. You can come up with others if you like. (Stay away from words that do not have the correct short A sound even though they begin with A – words like AUTO, ALIEN, and AHEAD.) Now ask him: "what does A say?" and let him answer.

Next, tell him E says something different from A. Get an egg from the refrigerator and ask him to guess what that sound is. If he says "egg" tell him it's only the first part of the word EGG, namely, /e/. Ask him if he can hear that same sound, /e/, at the start of these words: ELEPHANT, ENTER, END, ED, ELBOW, EXIT, EXTRA, ESCAPE, ECHO, EDGE, ENJOY, ENGINE, ELEVATOR, EMPTY, EVERY, ELEVEN, EXERCISE. Once he gets it, go back and review: "What does A say? What does E say?"

In a similar manner, teach him the sounds of I, O, and U. Tell him what these sounds are and ask if he can hear the sound in some words. Here are suggestions:

- For I: in, igloo, iguana, if, imp, itch, insect, inch, ignore, inside, invent, India, Italy, ink, icky, ill

- For O: ox, octopus, October, otter, olive, odd, omelet, object, opposite, ostrich, oxygen, opera, obstacle
- For U: up, umbrella, ugly, under, uncle, usher, us, udder, ulcer, ump, unfair, unless, ugh!

To review,

whenever you ask him:	what you want to hear is:
"What does A say?"	the first sound in the word AT
"What does E say?"	the first sound in the word EGG
"What does I say?"	the first sound in the word IN
"What does O say?"	the first sound in the word OX
"What does U say?"	the first sound in the word UP

It doesn't matter if this process takes 2 days or 30 days. These 5 sounds are crucial. Everything you'll do through Stage 9 depends on his quick familiarity with them. Review them with him throughout the day. Sometimes ask for them one at a time; other times ask for them all at once: /a/ /e/ /i/ /o/ /u/. Don't always do them in the same order. Reverse roles and let him ask you what these letters say. Give an occasional wrong answer and see if he corrects you. Sometimes, ask the question in reverse: "What letter says /e/?" and so on. Make it a game and keep it fun, but keep at it until he knows these 5 sounds thoroughly.

Next, tell her she needs to learn what 3 more letters say – and then she's going to start reading. That should keep her motivated! The 3 letters, mentioned earlier, are M, N, and S. Try to keep a single, common word associated with each letter as an aid for your child to remember the correct sound. I suggest the following:

A	apple
E	egg (or elephant)
I	igloo (or iguana)
O	ox (or otter)
U	umbrella (or underwear)
M	man (or moose)
N	nose
S	snake

Point out to your child that the name of each of these 3 letters (EM, EN, and ESS) has, embedded in it, exactly what each letter says:

EM says MMMMM (M says /m/)
EN says NNNNN (N says /n/)

ESS says SSSSS (S says /s/)

Here are some words that have the target sounds:

- S: sun, soup, Santa, sip, step, spin, see, slurp, stick, smile
- M: me, my, mouse, man, map, mad, middle, munch, mist
- N: no, never, new, net, near, nickel, napkin, news, nest

You'll find your child masters these 3 new sounds quickly compared to the 5 vowel sounds. Once you are sure she knows all 8 sounds, it's time to start blending and reading!

Now, not only does your child recognize the upper and lowercase versions of A, E, I, O, U, M, N, and S (from Stage 1), he knows what these letters "say," and he knows a common word associated with each of them. Next, you're going to teach him how to blend the sounds of these 8 letters into one-syllable words. Initially, there are three questions I would like to discuss with you:

- How many one-syllable "words" can be formed with only 8 letters?
- How many of these "words" are actual words, and how many are only pseudo words?
- Is it worth blending sounds if the result is only a pseudo word?

Mathematically, it's easy to answer the first question. Let's assume a "word" will have this configuration: a consonant, followed by a vowel, followed by another consonant – CVC for short. For the first consonant, there are, currently, 4 possibilities: M, N, S, or a blank (no letter at all). For the vowel, there are 5 possibilities, and for the final consonant, 3 possibilities: M, N, or S. Therefore, the total number of CVC combinations, using these 8 letters, is 4 x 5 x 3, or 60 one-syllable words. I've listed these 60 "words" in Appendix A.

If you look at this appendix, you'll notice about half are actual words (in boldface), and the other half are only pseudo words. However, all 60 are embedded in more complex words. For example, MUN, by itself, is not a real word, but it's part of larger words, such as MUNCH and MUNDANE. In addition, two of the pseudo words (UN and NON) are important prefixes and one (NESS) is an important suffix. So, my answer to the third question (above) is a *qualified* "yes." Your child will blend pseudo words here, in Stage 2, because one of your main goals right now is to give her "blending" practice with sustainable sounds. However, there'll be no need to keep blending pseudo words after this stage; there will be more than enough real words to keep both of you busy!

Appendix A is for you, not for your child. <u>Important note</u>: The words SON, IS, and AS are not in boldface in the appendix. That's because all 3 are irregular words. They are irregular because, in the word SON, O says /u/. In the words AS and IS, the S says /z/. These are complications that you'll handle later. For now, SON should be pronounced exactly as it is in the word SONIC – with a short O. Both AS and IS should be pronounced exactly as they are in the words ASK and KISS – where S says /s/. Recall that you are keeping all irregularities out of the first 6 stages to create the illusion that reading is a perfectly logical activity. Notice that in the appendix, I used double S whenever it would make a pseudo word into an actual word. Let's get back to instruction...

To start teaching the skill of *blending*, pick words from Appendix A that are already in your child's vocabulary, like MAN, MEN, MISS, SUN, SAM, AM, IN, US, AN, MESS. In fact, you can begin with everyone's all-time favorite: MOM. Get a blank sheet of paper and sit at a table with your child. Write MOM on the paper but spread the letters out a bit:

M   O   M

Ask your child to make the sound of the letter *for as long as you're pointing to it*. This is possible for her because all our letter sounds, so far, are sustainable. Now point to the first M for about two seconds. When time is up, immediately point to the O for another 2 seconds, and then to the final M, for 2 seconds. Now do it all again, but this time point to each letter for *one* second. Then again for a *half*-second each. Now do it one last time, sweeping your finger smoothly across the letters. Does your child catch on that these 3 sounds, when blended together quickly, form the word MOM? If she does, congratulate her and tell her she just read her first word! (If, after many tries, she does *not* seem to be catching on to blending, see the box at the end of this stage.)

If she seems to get it, write the word MOM again, 3 times, on the paper, but this time in the normal way, reviewing uppercase, lowercase, and mixed case. The paper now looks like this:

M   O   M
MOM
mom
Mom

Make the point this is the word MOM and it can be written in any of these ways.

Now try a new word:

M   A   N

Point to each letter as you did for MOM, each time going a little faster. If she sees what's going on, write the word in the normal way:

M   A   N
MAN
man
Man

Get out your blank 3 x 5 index cards. On a single card, write "MOM" in uppercase on one side and "mom" in lowercase on the other. Use a magic marker for this, making it nice and large. Take a second card and do the same with MAN. Place these two cards to the side. While only 2 cards now, this stack will grow quickly as you progress through the stages.

Do MESS next. Set it up on paper this way:

M   E   SS

If he asks about the two S's, tell him sometimes words that end in the sound /s/ have one S, and sometimes they have two. If he persists in wanting to know *why*, tell him the double S means to hold the S sound a tiny bit longer. You don't want to make an exception of these double-S words! When you are done with MESS (as you did above), make up your 3rd index card.

Next, tell him you're going to take away the M from MAN and create a new word. Write this on the paper:

A   N

Ask him if he knows this word. He may know it immediately or you may have to help him with the pointing procedure from above. Once he knows it, write:

A   N
AN
an
An

Make a 4th index card. You'll use these index cards as flash cards for the purpose of review. Use this word in some sentences for him. Don't write them on paper; do this verbally:

> "I would like to have AN apple."
> "AN alligator just ran through our kitchen."
> "She dropped AN egg on the floor."

In general, if you are not sure your child understands a word, discuss it with him and use it in some (amusing) sentences. See if he can come up with his own sentence. At this point you might also tell him the word AN, with two N's (ANN) is a common girl's name.

Next do SAM in the usual way, and after that, eliminate the S, for the word AM. Discuss these two words and use them in sentences as well. Now you have 6 flash cards. Mix them up and see if he knows all six. Help as needed. Note, he's not memorizing these words, he's reading them based on his knowledge of the sounds of the component letters. This is precisely what distinguishes phonics from Whole Word methods.

Over the next period of time (it doesn't matter how long), go through all 60 "words" in Appendix A with your child. Do the words he knows first. Then do the words he probably doesn't know, like SIN and NUN. (I sure knew these 2 words in Catholic grade school in the 50's!) This will give you the opportunity to teach him some new vocabulary. Define words that are new for him and use them in colorful sentences. Finally, do the pseudo words. If he can read SEN now, in Stage 2, then reading SEND and SENT in Stage 3 will be trivial for him. Similarly, if he can read NUM now, he'll more easily read NUMBER and STERNUM later. When he reads something that is not an actual word, tell him a "big" word that *does* use that sound (see Appendix A for suggestions).

Teacher Note: In no stage beyond this one will it be necessary for you to ask your child to read pseudo words. You're doing so here because there are only 60 "words" possible with his 8-letter toolkit and because the *primary* skill you are trying to teach in this stage is the blending of individual sounds. Practicing this skill is independent of whether the result is an actual word. Also, I have shown all 60 "words" are important parts of longer words he'll eventually need to read.

You're done with this stage when your child can read all 60 flash cards without struggling. This will take time. However, the blending skill learned here will be invaluable to what follows. It's doubtful any of the succeeding stages will take as long as Stage 2. I'll end this stage by trying to anticipate some questions you may have:

- As a stand-alone word, SON is pronounced the same as the word SUN. At this stage in the program, however, it should be pronounced so it rhymes with CON (short O). You don't want to deal with exceptions this early. For the time being, O *always* says /o/.
- You may find, at some point, it becomes unnecessary to spread out the letters on a piece of paper and point to them individually. If this happens, you can simply write the word on the index card directly and let your child sound it out on his own. This is a good sign!
- Both AS and ASS are actual words in English. Whether you present your child the single-S version or the double-S version, he should pronounce it only one way: as in the words ASTEROID or PASS. At this point in the

program, S says only /s/, not /z/. If you choose to deal with the actual word ASS, then you can share as many of its multiple meanings with your child as you see fit: a member of the horse family, a foolish person, slang for buttocks.

- Often in English, S's are doubled at the end of a word. I didn't double all of them because SIS and US are actual words. Simply tell your child (for now) a final S is often doubled – and leave it at that.

- You are purposely avoiding the English words IS and AS (for now) because the S in those 2 words has a Z sound. This is not only an undesirable complication, but it's also a sound you have not yet covered. (You'll do so in Stage 7). For this reason, I recommend presenting both words to your child with the double S.

- The two and three-syllable words in the appendix marked as examples are definitely *not* for your child to read. They are there only to convince *you* that all 60 blended sounds are worth knowing.

- The English word ON is actually pronounced /aw/ + /n/, not /o/ + /n/. However, your child has heard and has used this word many times; simply help with the correct pronunciation. You don't want to make this simple word an exception.

- EN and EM are actual words but they are rarely used. Their definitions involve units of measurement in type-setting. I suggest you treat these two words (and ES) as words that are simply the names of the letters N, M, and S.

Teacher Note: If your child does *not* seem to be catching on to this process of blending sounds into words, wait a few months and try again. Brain development is variable in children and it may simply be that he is not yet ready to grasp this blending skill. During this time, be sure to keep his letter recognition skills sharp and continue reading to him.

Stage 3
The Sounds of D, G, P, T
Consonant Blends

Your child now knows how to spell 8 of the 41 sounds of English. (Alternately, we could say your child now knows how to sound 8 of the 26 letters in the alphabet.) In addition, he knows how to blend these sounds into words he understands. This is an enormous accomplishment for both of you. By any standard, he's a beginning reader.

You'll be adding only 4 new letters (and their sounds) in this stage, but that will greatly expand the number of words your child can decode. To see why this is so, consider the fact that the 60 "words" in Stage 2 had either the structure VC or CVC (where V stands for vowel sound and C for consonant sound). Now you'll be expanding your child's toolkit to 12 sounds: the 8 already mastered plus the 4 new sounds: /d/, /g/, /p/, and /t/. With these 4 newcomers, however, words having *consonant blends* become a possibility: 4 beginning blends (SM, SN, ST, and SP), as well as 7 ending blends (ST, SP, MP, ND, NT, PT, and MPT). I've listed all of the consonant blends in Appendix R.

So, besides the simple VC and CVC structures the 2 of you looked at in the previous stage, you'll now help him decode more complex structures like CCVC (STOP), CVCC (DAMP), and CCVCC (STAND). You might be wondering how many single-syllable "words" are possible now, with these 4 new letters? Let's do the math again. To begin the word, we can choose from 7 single consonants, 4 beginning consonant blends, or a blank (total: 12). For the middle of the word, we still choose from among 5 vowels. For the end of the word, we can pick from 7 single consonants and 7 ending consonant blends (total: 14). Therefore, the total number of possible "words" expands to 12 x 5 x 14 = 840 possibilities! This is a huge jump from the 60 possible words in Stage 2.

This math dictates I not attempt to list all possible "words," including pseudo words, as I did in Stage 2. If you look at Appendix B, you'll see I list only that subset of these 840 possibilities that are real words. There are about 160 of them. Since from this point on you'll be looking only at real words with your child, you may want to toss out the 30 or so pseudo words from the flash card stack you already have. In this stage, you'll gradually be adding up to 160 new words to that stack. The reason I say "up to" 160 is that your child can master the new sounds and the new consonant blends in this stage without covering every single word in Appendix B. You may wish to eliminate some of the more obscure words like TAD, SOD, and SUMP. Doing so will not have any serious effect on the learning process. I hope, however, you'll use the opportunity to continue expanding your child's vocabulary.

You probably noticed none of these 4 new sounds are sustainable. Therefore, the method from the previous stage, of pointing to a letter for a second or two while your child makes its sound, *won't work here.* That's okay. It simply means you'll now start teaching the topic of blending in a different manner.

What, exactly, does D say? Well, it says the *first* sound you can hear in each of the following words: DAN, DEN, DIP, DOT, DUG. What is that sound? Traditional phonics holds that "D says duh," but that's neither accurate nor helpful. "Duh" is the combination /d/ + /u/. To teach the child D says "duh" is useful if the word he is trying to decode is DUCK. However, if the word is DAD, DECK, or DOUGHNUT, "duh" is unhelpful, even misleading.

Let's plan to deal with this problem directly. With non-sustainable sounds starting to appear, I suggest you now start teaching your child, that to decide what a consonant says, she should always look at the vowel that *follows* it. In other words, you won't ask her "what does D say?" because D's sound can't be sustained and it's difficult to answer such a question accurately. Instead, you'll ask "what are the *sounds* of D?" The answer you'll want is /da/, /de/, /di/, /do/, and /du/ – the D sound blended with each of the 5 short vowel sounds she already knows so well. (I am using /da/ as shorthand for /d/ + /a/; /de/ as shorthand for /d/ + /e/, and so on.)

The idea here is that when she attempts to decode a word like DEN, she won't think "duh + eh + nnn" (trying to blend 3 sounds, one of which, duh, is incorrect), but simply "/de/ + /n/." Since she already knows the 5 short vowel sounds, /a/ /e/ /i/ /o/ /u/, it's a simple *additional* step to ask her for those 5 sounds with the D attached to them: /da/ /de/ /di/ /do/ /du/. You'll see how easy this will make the blending she must do later in this stage. Keep in mind that at this point in the program, /do/ is not to be pronounced as in the sentence "DO your work," but as it is in the word DOT, with a short O sound. The word DO, an exception, will be covered later.

Ok, let's get back to your child. In this stage, she first needs to understand the fundamental difference between a *vowel* and a *consonant.* After reviewing the 5 vowel sounds with her, tell her A, E, I, O, and U are the most important letters in the alphabet. Give her a book (or magazine or newspaper) and ask her to look at as many words as she pleases. Does she see *why* these 5 letters are so important? If not, help her out: every word she sees has at least one of these 5 letters. They are the most-used letters (and the most-used sounds) in our language. Tell her we call them "vowels." Let her look at the flash cards from Stage 2 to verify that all the words she already reads have a vowel. Explain that all the other letters in the alphabet are called "consonants." Remind her she already knows all 5 vowel sounds and 3 consonant sounds; then let her know what's coming next: the 4 new sounds of the consonants P, T, D, and G.

Teacher Note: One might argue that to teach a child D+O says /d/ + /o/, as in the word DOT, only to later teach him D+O says /d/ + /ew/, as in DO YOUR WORK, is poor pedagogy: we're teaching something now that will later have to be unlearned. That's not the case. D+O says /d/ + /o/ in many words such as DOCK, DON, DOT, DOLLAR, DOMINATE, DODGE, DOFF, and ADOPT. D+O also commonly says /d/ + /O/ (long O) in words like DONOR, DONUT, DOMESTIC, DONATE, DOSE, AVOCADO, TORNADO, and TORPEDO. In fact, the *least* common way to pronounce D+O is /d/ + /ew/ as in the common English word DO. The word DO is an exception that will be covered in Stage 9. The mismatch between the sounds and the letters in the word DO is serious enough that DO is on the Tricky 50 list in Appendix S.

Start her off with the letter P. Tell her you'll say some words that start with the P sound and she should listen closely. As you speak these words, exaggerate the sound of P: PICKLE, POT, PENCIL, PAN, PINK, PRETZEL, PIZZA, PEE, PUZZLE. Next, tell her you have 5 words that start *and* end with P: PEP, POP, PEEP, PUMP, POOP. Now ask her: What do you think P says?

Her response is likely to be a combination of the P sound and some vowel. If she says "peh," tell her that sounds like P with an E attached: /pe/. If she says "puh," tell her that sounds like P with a U attached: /pu/. It's difficult to isolate the P sound from the vowel sound that follows it. As the 2 of you try to do so, the sound of P becomes almost inaudible – like a puff of air. Discuss this fact with her, as well as the fact that the P sound, unlike the M, N, and S sounds, is *not* sustainable. (We can't hold on to it. It quickly disappears!)

Now, hold up an index card with the 5 vowels spread out from left to right:

a　　e　　i　　o　　u

Reviewing, ask her for all five sounds. She's an expert on these by now, so her verbal response is: /a/ /e/ /i/ /o/ /u/. Now hold up a second index card with the following written on it:

pa　pe　pi　po　pu

and ask, "What does P say with the vowels attached?" or "What are the 5 sounds of P?" What you want to hear, of course, is /pa/ /pe/ /pi/ /po/ /pu/. Help her, if necessary, get to the 5 correct sounds. She simply needs to attach that puff of air – the P sound – to the vowel sounds she already knows. Correct her if she says any of these sounds using 2 syllables, for instance, saying "puh, ah" instead of simply /pa/ for the first one. What you want to hear from her is PAT, PET, PIT, POT, PUTT – but without that final T sound. (Reminder: /a/ is the first sound in "apple," not the sound you hear in the word PASTA.)

Prepare similar index cards for M, N, and S:

ma	me	mi	mo	mu
na	ne	ni	no	nu
sa	se	si	so	su

M, N, and S are the consonants the 2 of you did in Stage 2. Their sounds are sustainable. However, going forward, you want her to *habitually* notice the vowel following the consonant before deciding what a consonant "says," even when that consonant is sustainable.

When you hold up the M card, ask her for *all* the sounds of M. What you want to hear is /ma/ /me/ /mi/ /mo/ /mu/ (MAD, MED, MID, MOD, MUD but without the final /d/ sound). Coach her as much as necessary to get to this point. It shouldn't take long. <u>Note</u>: ME, of course, is an English word, but that is *not* the pronunciation you want here. Here you want /m/ + /e/: the sound of the word MET but without the T. You'll get to the word ME in Stage 8. Now hold up the N and S cards you prepared above, one at a time, and see if she responds correctly:

/na/ /ne/ /ni/ /no/ /nu/   and   /sa/ /se/ /si/ /so/ /su/

Same word of caution here: NO and SO are English words. Nonetheless, you want her to pronounce them with the short O sound – as in the words KNOB and SOB.

Now, what you did above with the letter P, you can do with the remaining 3 letters: D, G, and T (DEE, JEE, and TEE). For D and T, the name of the letter contains its sound; for G, that's not the case. Take all the time you need. Choose some good words that start with these letters to introduce your child to the new sounds. Here are some suggestions:

- G: girl, goose, gift, gum, get, gap, gas, grief, game, God, giggle, gust, gal (but not GEM or GYPSY or any other word where the G has a J sound! You won't cover that situation until Stage 17).
- D: dog, dad, dirt, danger, Dan, doughnut, dinosaur, dip, don't, damp, done, dead.
- T: Tom, tap, tender, tip, tree, turtle, toy, tent, trip, top, taste, tooth, tub, tiny, two.

Once you introduce each of these new sounds, prepare index cards similar to the ones you did above:

ga	ge	gi	go	gu
da	de	di	do	du
ta	te	ti	to	tu

As you hold up the card, ask for the 5 sounds of the letter. Again, note that GO, TO, and DO are actual English words. For now, however, your child should pronounce all of them with a short O sound (as in GOT, TOT, and DOT). The English words GO, TO, and DO are exceptions and you'll deal with them later. Remember, you're treating English as 100% logical and without exceptions here in the early going.

You probably realize your child won't need these specially prepared 5-sound cards for long. It's easy throughout the day to simply ask your child for *all* the sounds of any of the consonants already covered. Again, encourage her to quiz you as well. You are finished with the above when your child knows the 5 sounds of each consonant covered so far: M, N, S, D, P, T, and G. Take all the time you need.

Now, look again at Appendix B. Initially, you'll focus only on the CVC words with your child; you can do the VC words and the consonant blends later. There are about 90 such CVC words. (Notice that words in Appendix B, like PASS and PUTT, are listed with the CVC group instead of the CVCC group. That's because SS and TT are not blends. They represent a single sound. All the words in the CVC category have exactly 3 sounds.) Eliminate some words if you wish, and then place the rest on index cards as before: lowercase on one side and upper on the other. Hold up one such card for your child – let's say it's the one with PET written on it – but hold the card in such a way as to hide the T with your finger. Your child should say /pe/ as a *single syllable*, correctly blending /p/ and /e/. (This is precisely what you were practicing when you asked him for the 5 sounds of P.) Your job is to make sure it's the correct single syllable. Now take your finger off the T and ask him to read the whole word. What does he do?

- Does he read the word PET and recognize it as such? If so, congratulate him and move to the next word.
- Does he *not* recognize the word because he holds the PE sound too long before he adds the sound of the T, making it sound like a two-syllable word? (He can do this because the E sound is sustainable.) Tell him to speed it up!
- Does he say PET smoothly as a single pulse of sound, but still look confused? Define the word PET for him! Tell him he's done it!

Let's say the next card has the word MUD written on it. Show it to him with the D covered. He says /mu/ as a single syllable (/m/ + /u/). You reveal the D and he says MUD.

Plan, at least initially, to go through all the CVC words from Appendix B in the above manner. I say "initially" because at some point, it may become clear he no longer needs you to hide that last letter from him. He can simply read the whole word at once, the way you and I do. I suggest you test him after 20 words or so. Hold up the card with the next new word, but this time without the last letter hidden. Ask him if he can simply do all the blending silently, in his head, and then say the whole word as a single sound. If he has trouble with this, go back to hiding the last letter with your finger for another 20 words.

Stop whenever you sense he's tired. The following day, review the Stage 3 cards he has already successfully decoded. Until he can read the whole CVC word as a single pulse of sound, the blending should always be CV + C. (The first consonant and the vowel as a single sound, blended with the final letter.) Define and discuss words as necessary, then have your child use the word in a sentence to be sure he understands it. Take the time to build vocabulary. When you finish with the CVC words, do the 10 or so VC words next. Three of them are high-frequency words: UP, AT, IT. These 3 words (plus DID) combined with US, AM, AN, IN, and ON from Stage 2, give your child 9 of the most frequent words in English. High-frequency words are always boxed in the appendices.

In doing these short VC words, you don't have to hide the last letter. Since these words start with a vowel, he can hold that initial sound for as long as he wants. When he gets tired of holding it, he need only make the sound of the second letter. Tell him to speed up and he'll be saying the word automatically!

Finally, you can focus on the consonant blends in Appendix B. Your child is ready to do these only if she has reached the point of being able to handle most of the CVC words in Appendices A and B *without* the help of you covering up the last letter. In other words, she can read these CVC words like you and I read them – not as fast certainly, and with some hesitancy no doubt – but she can read most of them as a single, smooth sound.

If she is not yet at this point, delay moving on until she masters this skill. You have over 100 CVC (and VC) words on index cards from Appendices A and B. Review these with her. Perhaps, more importantly, review the 5 sounds of each of the consonants M, N, S, P, T, D, and G.

For the consonant blends in Appendix B, you'll be hiding letters with your finger again – but in a different manner than above. Place these words on flash cards as usual. Keep the double blends (CCVCC) for last. Explain to your child she has not yet blended two consonants together (and she must learn this because it happens a lot!). Two consonants that flow together easily are S and T. Can she guess how ST might sound? Whether she can or not, show her an index card with one of the words from the *beginning* ST group in the appendix. (There is an ending ST group there as well.) Let's say you pick the word STEP. Show her the word with the S covered by your finger. Now, for her, it's simply another run-of-the-mill CVC word. At this point, she should be good at these, so she reads TEP. Now reveal the S and ask her to read the entire word smoothly and quickly: STEP. If she doesn't recognize the word, it's because she is holding the S sound too long!

Now, do the same with the word STOP. Have her first read the CVC word TOP. Once she does, reveal the S: STOP. Having read these two words, does she see how easily S and T blend together? Is the sound of ST as she predicted? Tell her most consonants do not blend nicely at all. Have some fun with her trying to blend MN or DG – it can't be done without inserting a vowel. Can she read the rest of the beginning ST group without help? If not, keep hiding the initial S. Do the other groups of beginning blends (SM-, SN-, and SP-) in the same manner.

For the various groups of *final* blends, do the opposite of the above. Let's say you pick the word SEND from the -ND group. Now you'll cover the *final* letter, D, so he can again focus, as he did above, on the simple CVC sound, SEN. (This is one of the pseudo words from Stage 2.) Once he gets it, uncover the last letter: SEND. Help by covering letters with your finger only for as long as he needs this aid. Discuss unfamiliar words and use them in sentences to help build his vocabulary. Cycle through all the ending blends in the same manner. You'll notice your child starting to get good at this.

Finally, tell your child there can be consonant blends at *both* ends of a word! He should find that exciting! There are 7 such words in the appendix. Take one of them, STAMP for instance, and hide *both* the S and the P with your fingers. He reads the CVC pseudo word: TAM. Show the S and he reads STAM – now show the P: STAMP. Do it the other way as well. After he reads TAM, show the P: TAMP. Then show the S: STAMP. It works either way. Enjoy the other six! For that single example of a three-letter consonant blend, TEMPT, start by showing the first 3 letters, then add P, then add the final T.

Since you'll continue using this stage's method through Stage 8, let's take the time to sum it up here:

- Using the flash cards you've been creating, spend the first 5 minutes of each lesson reviewing words your child already knows how to decode.
- Introduce the new consonant sound by saying words beginning with that sound – as you did with the letter P above.
- Make sure your child can express the target sound properly with each of the 5 short vowels, for example: /pa/ /pe/ /pi/ /po/ /pu/.
- Go to the appropriate appendix and begin with the CVC words, transferring each of them to their own flash cards. If he is having trouble with these CVC words, hide the last letter with your finger and help him read the CV part of the word as a *single syllable*. Thus, the vowel always informs how the beginning consonant is articulated. Once he does that, reveal the last letter and he should be able to read the entire word.
- Do the VC words. You don't need to hide letters for these short words.
- Do the consonant blends: CCVC, CVCC, or CCVCC. If he is having trouble with these words, allow him to see only the CVC part of the word. Once he reads that properly, show the other letter(s).
- Hide letters only if he is having trouble. The goal is to have him read without help; do whatever you can to move him toward this goal as soon as possible.

Stage 4
The Sounds of B, F, C/K
Spelling Begins

During this stage, you'll be adding 4 new letters and 3 new sounds to your child's phonics toolkit. In addition, you'll start asking him to spell simple words he can already read. Let's discuss the spelling first. It's possible to teach your child to read without ever once asking him to spell something. To do so, however, would be to waste a wonderful opportunity to provide him with an additional skill. I strongly recommend you include some daily spelling practice.

The Spelling Corner: Since you're teaching your child to read phonetically, teaching him to spell is an easy and valuable add-on to this program. Reading and spelling are reverse processes. As he spells, he encodes sound into text; as he reads, he decodes text back into sound. Starting here in Stage 4, take a little time (10-15 minutes per day) to spell with your child.

You can do this informally throughout the day, apart from the more formal reading lesson. When taking a walk, or having lunch, ask him: "Can you spell the word PET?" If he finds this difficult, exaggerate the two sounds (/pe/ + /t/) as you repeat the word. As you start out, keep to the simplest VC and CVC words in your stack of flash cards. Then, as he begins to get better at spelling, start including the CCVC and CVCC words. If necessary, help with the blends: "Can you spell TAM? Now can you spell TAMP? Now can you spell STAMP?" When you ask him to spell words like PASS, does he include the second S?

Naturally, ask him to spell only words having the sounds you've already covered. Here in Stage 4, ask your child to spell words only from Stages 2 and 3. Going forward, the words you use for spelling practice should always lag one stage behind the new words and sounds that are currently being studied. While working through Stage 5, you'll ask him to spell Stage 4 words, and so on. When he spells a word incorrectly, try to pronounce his mistaken spelling (if possible). This can help him see where he went wrong. You can also simply show him the flash card with the correct spelling.

If he is young, all the spelling can be done orally. If he is older, and he has the necessary motor skills, you can ask him to write the word on paper.

Before starting the new letters and sounds of this stage with your child, let's discuss the letters C and K because this is an unusual situation. These 2 letters often have the same sound, /k/, when they start a word: CAB, KEG, KID, COB, CUB. Note that when the vowel is E or I, the letter K is used to start the word, not C. In English, when C is followed by E or I, the C has an S sound, as in CITY or CENTER. If you were to spell KID with a C you would have to pronounce it SID as in the words LUCID and PLACID. This is a complication you'll handle later (Stage 17). For now, you still wish to sustain the illusion that English is 100% regular and logical. Note, too, that when the sound /k/ comes at the *end* of a word, C and K are used together to symbolize it: BACK, DUCK, NECK, KICK.

Ok, let's get back to reading instruction. Explain to your child the letters C and K have the same sound. If he asks why, tell him you don't know, or you'll explain later, or tell him the truth: the few people who could read and write in the past, pretty much spelled words any way they pleased. Then in 1806, Noah Webster published his first dictionary. In it, he attempted to reform and standardize English spelling. Many of the decisions he made were gradually adopted, including the way the letters C and K now interact. But do not (yet) explain that C can sometimes have an S sound – you'll do that in Stage 17.

The name of the letter K (KAY = /k/ + /A/) has the sound both C and K symbolize. Say some words that start with the K (or C) sound and tell him to listen: CAT, KETTLE, KIT, CORN, COB, CUT, CRAB, CREEPY, KEEP, COIN, KID. Here are some words that have the same C/K sound at the end: DUCK, BACK, QUICK, LICK, NECK, CLOCK.

Ask him if he can make the K sound himself. Help as needed. As soon as he seems to have the K sound in his head, ask him (without making any special cards this time) for the 5 sounds of K. Does he correctly say /ka/ /ke/ /ki/ /ko/ /ku/? (He should give the same answer for the 5 sounds of C.) Remind him the sound of a consonant depends on the vowel that follows it. This may be an appropriate time to review the 5 sounds of the earlier consonants from Stages 2 and 3.

Now do the same for the letters F (EFF = /e/ + /f/) and B (BEE = /b/ + /E/). Again, the names of these two letters contain the sound the letters symbolize. Here are some suggested words for introducing them to your child:

- F: fix, fat, fun, frog, friend, farm, feet, fog, fire, stuff, puff, cliff, life, laugh
- B: boy, box, bed, bean, bite, bug, bag, bone, brown, job, rib, gab

Once he knows the 5 sounds of both F and B, ask him which of these new sounds is sustainable. Take some time now to review *all* the consonant sounds to date. This is important because the new words in Appendix C mix all those consonant sounds together. Before asking him to read those words, make sure he is confident about the 5 sounds of each of these consonants: M, N, S, D, G, P, T, F, B, and C/K.

Approach the new words in Appendix C much as you did in the last stage. (See the summary in the box at the end of Stage 3). Take special note of the following:

- A few words have an exclamation point. I called them "excitement marks" with my children and told them it means they should read the word with emotion.
- Point out that words starting with the sound /k/ sometimes use C and sometimes use K – but a word ending in the sound /k/ is always spelled CK.
- CK is not a blend; it spells a single sound: /k/.
- Once you finish Appendix C with your child, he'll already be able to read well over 300 words!
- Ending F sounds are usually spelled FF, much like the double S in Stage 2.
- Upon finishing Stage 4, take the 300 or so index cards you've made from the words in appendices A, B, and C and review them with your child. If you notice any problems, go back and spend time with that issue.
- The only new consonant blends in this stage are the beginning blends SK- and SC-, and the ending blends, -SK, -CT, and -FT.
- I placed CANT, without an apostrophe, in the appendix. You'll cover contractions (with proper apostrophes) in Stage 17. Until that time, I see no harm here; it's a word he uses all the time, and it's perfectly phonetic.

Stage 5
The Sound of L

You'll be adding only a single letter and sound in this stage. That's because the letter L adds 13 new consonant blends: 7 beginning blends (BL, CL, FL, GL, PL, SL, SPL) and 6 ending blends (LT, LF, LM, LP, LD, LK). If you examine Appendix D, you'll see this single sound, /l/, adds 150 more words your child, with a little practice, will easily read.

The Spelling Corner: Spelling during this stage should focus on words from Stage 4. Remind your child that words ending in the sound /f/ are spelled FF, words ending in the sound /s/ are spelled SS, and words ending in /k/ are spelled CK. Expect spelling mistakes on words beginning with the sound /k/: should they be spelled with a C or a K? I recommend that, since you are still in the English-is-regular phase of this program, you accept either spelling. If that does not appeal to you, you can tell her to use K when the following vowel is an E or an I.

Let's get started. The name of the consonant L (ELL = /e/ + /l/) has the sound which L symbolizes. Introduce it by asking your child to listen to some L words: LOVE, LAUGH, LACE, LICORICE, LIKE, LIP, LAP, LATER, LITTLE, SPILL, FILL, BALL. Can she tell you the sound? Ask her if the sound can be sustained (held). Then ask for the five sounds: /la/ /le/ /li/ /lo/ /lu/.

Once she is clear on the new sound, transfer the CVC words in Appendix D to flash cards. Can she read most of them without much help? Point out that words ending in L usually have a double L.

There are a lot of consonant blends in Appendix D. Weed out the more obscure words if you like, and then, using the template at the end of Stage 3, see how she does. Discuss with her how easily the L sound blends with many other consonants. Only if necessary should you use your fingers to hide letters on the flash cards. SPLINT is an unusual word with a CCCVCC structure. If she has trouble, start with LIN (the CVC part of the word) and then reveal the other 3 letters, one at a time.

Stage 6
The Sound of R

Just as you did in Stage 5, you'll be adding only a single letter and sound in this stage. That's because R, like L, blends with so many other consonants. In this case, there are a total of 26 such blends: 10 beginning blends (BR, CR, DR, FR, GR, TR, PR, SCR, SPR, STR) and 16 ending blends (RB, RD, RF, RG, RK, RL, RM, RN, RP, RT, RST, RCH, RSH, RTH, RVE, and RSE).

For now, however, you need only do the 10 beginning blends with your child. The reason is, when an R *follows* a vowel, it automatically changes the sound of the vowel. You can hear this for yourself if you compare the vowel sound in each of the following pairs of words:

cat	car
hen	her
sit	sir
not	nor
fun	fur

For the first word in each of the above pairs, the vowel has the short sound the two of you have been working on since Stage 2. However, for the second word in each pair, not a single vowel has its short sound. When R follows a vowel, you get some new vowel sounds that are neither long nor short. These new sounds, /ar/, /or/, and /er/, are among the 41 elemental sounds of English listed in Table 1 and in Appendix P. We'll cover these new sounds, and the above *ending* blends, in Stage 13. So why aren't /ir/ and /ur/ included on the list of 41 English sounds? They're not unique. You can verify this fact by noting that HER, SIR, and FUR all rhyme. Thus, /er/ = /ir/ = /ur/.

> **The Spelling Corner**: Spelling can now focus on the L words from Stage 5. Remind her that most words ending in the sound /l/ are spelled LL. Also, the blended sound /k/ + /l/ is always spelled CL (CLASS, CLAP), not KL. As usual, if she has trouble spelling blends (like PLANT), ask her to spell only the CVC part of the word (LAN). Then ask her to spell PLAN and, finally, PLANT.

Look at Appendix E. There aren't a lot of CVC words, but there are 120 words that begin with new R blends or end with blends you've already seen. To introduce the sound, have your child listen for the sound of R in the words RUN, RIP, RED, RUG, ROCK, RAILROAD, READ, REACH, ROPE, RAIN, RAKE, RIDE. Once she is pronouncing /r/ correctly, ask her if the sound of R is sustainable.

Does she volunteer the 5 sounds of R without you even having to ask at this point: /ra/ /re/ /ri/ /ro/ /ru/? Once she is sure of these 5 sounds, she should be able to read the 20 or so CVC words in the appendix without too much difficulty. Just help with any new vocabulary.

The consonant blends are going to take some time. If she is struggling with these words, you have no choice but to move slowly, covering letters to isolate the CVC sound existing in every one of them. There's no rush. The goal is to have her read well; don't worry about time.

On the other hand, your child might be racing through these words so fast it seems to you a waste of time to transfer the words to flash cards. In this case, you might consider having your child read the words directly from the appendix. You must make this call. If you do have her read words directly from the appendix, I recommend a test at the end: pick two words from each of the blend groups (BR, CR, DR and so on), place those words on index cards, shuffle, and see how she does reading them under these circumstances.

Teacher Note: Here's something you may find interesting. (I sure do!) For each of the 5 pairs of words at the beginning of this stage, the initial consonant is the same, but the vowel sound following that consonant is different. Now, note the shape of your mouth and lips as you prepare to say the word HEN. Do the same for the word HER. Note, even *before* you make that initial H sound, your mouth and lips are in a different configuration for these two words. Amazing, no? The same is true for each of these 5 pairs of words.

This phenomenon is not due to the presence of the R (compare HIM and HOT and you'll notice it as well). Instead, it's a tribute to the speed and power of the human brain. For skilled readers, the brain registers every letter in a word at once, matches the letters with appropriate sounds, and then, on an *unconscious* level, gets our mouth, lips, and tongue ready to coarticulate the 3 sounds into a single pulse of sound: HOT.

This is one of the main reasons you've been training your child to look at the vowel *following* a consonant before deciding how to pronounce that consonant. You're training her to do consciously, something that will soon become utterly automatic for her. This is a good example of the power of phonics!

Stage 7
The Sounds of H, J, Q, V, W, X, Y, Z

Only one sound in each of the prior two stages and now eight sounds in a single stage! As you probably recognize, these are among the less frequent consonant sounds in the English language. In addition, some of these letters are restricted to only the beginning or end of a word. English words don't end in J, Q or V, and only a few obscure words start with X. While many words end in Y, you'll postpone looking at them until Stage 14 because, for those words, Y acts as a vowel, not as a consonant: BOY, DAY, EARLY. Similarly, in Stage 13, you'll see that a final W also acts as a vowel: LAW, FEW, COW, SNOW. H is an important and frequent letter, but this is due to its combined sound with S (SHIP), with C (CHIP), and with T (THINK). These two-letter combinations (SH, CH, and TH) will be covered shortly, in Stage 8.

By postponing the above complications until later stages, you'll be able to sustain the illusion that English is regular through most of this stage. The topics you'll teach here include:

- Words that begin with H, J, V, W, Y, and Qu
- Words that begin or end with Z
- Words that end in X
- Some new beginning consonant blends: SW, TW, DW, SQU
- Words that start with WR, WH, or KN (these are not blends)
- Four high-frequency words in which a final S has a Z sound

The Spelling Corner: During this stage, focus your spelling practice on the words from Stage 6. Remind your child these will all be R words and she can expect lots of beginning R blends. Consider doing related words together: have her spell RUM, then RUMP, GRUMP, and TRUMP. RICK, followed by BRICK, PRICK, and TRICK. Tell her you're going to have her spell three words that differ only in the vowel: TRICK, TRACK, TRUCK and RAMP, ROMP, RUMP. By doing such spelling exercises, you're teaching her to listen closely to individual sounds, and you're increasing her sound-awareness.

As I mentioned in Chapter 2, X does not have a unique sound; it's simply shorthand for the ending consonant blend KS (SIX = SIKS, FOX = FOKS). Also, the letter Q, always accompanied by U, is simply an alternate way of spelling the beginning consonant blend KW (QUIZ = KWIZ, QUEST = KWEST).

The consonant combinations WR, WH, and KN are not blends because each of them spells only a single sound:

- For WR, the W is silent. WR says /r/ (WRIST).
- For WH, the H is silent. WH says /w/ (WHEN).
- For KN, the K is silent. KN says /n/ (KNOB).

Let's discuss how you might approach the above topics with your child. Ignoring Q and X for the time being, you can start this stage by introducing her to the sounds of 6 new letters: H, J, V, W, Y, and Z. Here are some suggested words to help in that process:

- H: hat, hot, hello, happy, hen, hippopotamus, hope, hug
- J: jelly, juice, jet, jar, jam, Jack, Jill, job, jug, jazz, jerk
- V: van, vest, very, vine, visit, vanilla, voice, volcano
- W: wet, win, worm, wing, walnut, wipe, wise, wall, week
- Y: yard, yellow, yes, yell, year, yawn, yuck, yodel, yum
- Z: zoo, zebra, zipper, zero, zest, zap, zone, buzz, fizz, snooze, sneeze, jazz

Tell her the names of the letters V (VEE), J (JAY), and Z (ZEE) each contain the sound the letter symbolizes. (The names of the other 3 letters are no help whatsoever!) As usual, make sure she can give you the 5 sounds for each of these 6 consonants:

/ha/ /he/ /hi/ /ho/ /hu/
/ja/ /je/ /ji/ /jo/ /ju/...   and so on.

When you're sure she knows these 6 sounds thoroughly, do the CVC words with her from Appendix F, followed by the consonant blends. I think you know the drill by now. Once she can read all the words on the first page of the appendix, continue with what is below.

Now, with the Z sound fresh in her mind, introduce 4 key words that have a slightly different spelling than she might imagine. Have her read these 4 "words" from a single index card:

ISS   HISS   ASS   HASS

ASS is a word from Stage 2 and HISS is the sound of a snake. The other two are pseudo words. Tell her if we simply drop an S from each of these words, we get 4 new words in English. On the same index card, write them out:

ISS   HISS   ASS   HASS
IS   HIS   AS   HAS

Explain that for these important words, the final (single) S has a Z sound. Knowing this odd fact (or so it must seem to her!), can she read these words correctly? Have her use each in a sentence. (You might also discuss with her how odd it is that these words are not spelled IZZ, HIZZ, AZZ, and HAZZ. Explain that, sometimes, English spelling is a little tricky.) These are high-frequency words that show up everywhere; make sure she knows them well. (Consider posting these 4 words together in a place where she will often see them for review.)

The only topics remaining in this stage are grouped together in the box marked "Some Anomalies" in Appendix F. You've reached the point where you can no longer sustain the illusion that English is a regular language, with a simple one-to-one correspondence between letters and sounds. Just above, you showed your child S can have a Z sound. Now the two of you are going to look, not only at "silent" letters, but at a Q that sounds like the blend KW, and an X that sounds like the blend KS. Reading is about to become more interesting and more challenging!

But look at how far you have brought your child with this carefully constructed illusion. He can read over a thousand words, and better yet, he is convinced reading makes sense and is rational, and better still, he is sure he can do it and it's fun! He is adept at blending sounds. Looking at some complications and anomalies now will barely slow him down. It's time to start showing him all the complexities of the English language.

Let's continue with the box marked "Some Anomalies" in Appendix F. Ask her if she can name the only 2 letters in the alphabet the 2 of you have not yet discussed (X and Q). To help her master the sound of X, show her this "word" on an index card:

FOK

She should be able to read this simple CVC construction. Now add an S to it and let her read the word:

FOKS

Does she recognize the word? After agreeing with her that it's a small, furry animal, tell her the little critter *could* be spelled this way – perhaps *should* be spelled this way – but, in fact, it's incorrect. It's spelled FOX. Write it on the same index card:

FOKS
FOX

Tell her X is *often* used to take the place of the KS blend. In other words, for reading purposes, X = KS. Take a moment to help her *spell* the name of the letter X: EKS. Now she can see the name of the letter (EKS) contains the letter's sound (/k/ + /s/). Help her pronounce KS correctly: the word FIX minus the /f/ and /i/ sounds.

Do the above FOX exercise again, but with MIK, MIKS, MIX and with SIK, SIKS, SIX. Now place all the X words from the appendix on index cards and see if she can read them without the above help. You may have to define some of these words for her. For the words, NEXT and TEXT, it might be helpful if you initially hide the final T with your finger.

If she asks *why* English replaces KS with X, congratulate her for asking such an excellent question, and do one of 3 things:

- Admit you don't know,
- Tell her it's time for lunch, or
- Make up a story along these lines: English is sometimes unfathomable! We must live with these charming oddities!

It's important for her to know X does not *always* replace KS. Show her this "word" on a card:

STIX

Given what she has just done, she'll probably read it correctly and say STICKS. Now give her the bad news: the correct spelling is STICKS, not STIX. In this word, we do *not* replace the KS with X.

STIX
STICKS

She may now ask the obvious question: When can X replace KS, and when can it *not* do so? The simplest answer is that we can't use X to form the *plural* of something. (You'll need to define "plural" here as "more than one"). Tell her English uses S, not X, to form the plural and give her some examples: POT/POTS, HAT/HATS, LIP/LIPS, and STICK/STICKS – not STIX!

If she still seems confused by all this X craziness, write the following word on a card and tell her the situation is (let her read it):

COM-PLEX

Now move on to the last letter: Q. To help him master the sound of Q, show him this word on an index card: WIT. He should be able to read this simple CVC blend. Now write the word again, but with a K at the beginning and let him read it: KWIT. Does he recognize the word? Now give him the surprising news: no word in English starts with the spelling KW. If an English word starts with the blended sound, /k/ + /w/, the correct spelling is (write it on the same card) QU:

> WIT
> KWIT
> QUIT

Agree with him that this is perplexing situation in English – but we're stuck with it. Point out that Q is *always* attached to its buddy, U, and that QU is the correct spelling of the sound /kw/. In other words, for reading purposes, QU = KW.

Do another one with him. Write WACK on a card and let him read it. Then write it again, but with a beginning K: KWACK. Does he recognize the word? When he does, see if you can get the correct spelling from him:

> WACK
> KWACK
> QUACK

To combine the last two lessons, show him a card with the following 4 phrases:

> DUX KWACK
> DUX QUACK
> DUCKS KWACK
> DUCKS QUACK

After agreeing that all 4 phrases say the same thing, discuss with him which one is correct and why. (The last one is correct because no English word starts with KW and because X can't be used to form the plural. Boston Red Sox fans will undoubtedly disagree!)

Next, place the dozen or so QU words from the appendix on index cards (spelled correctly) and see if he can read them without the above help. You may have to define some of these words for him. If he asks *why* English replaces KW with QU, see above for 3 possible answers. If he has trouble with any of these words, like SQUID for instance, replace the QU with KW on a card:

> SQUID
> SKWID

Cover the SK and let him read the CVC word WID. Uncover the K: KWID. Uncover the S: SKWID. Define the word (if needed) and remind him that in English, QU always replaces KW.

Finally, introduce him to "silent" letters. This is a large topic. As you know, a silent E at the end of a word often changes that word's pronunciation and meaning. (You'll see this in Stage 11). What you are after here, however, is the less frequent situation of silent letters at the *beginning* of a word. Start by showing him the word WRIST on an index card. It's likely he can't read it. Discuss with him the fact that WR can't be a consonant blend because there is no way to blend those 2 individual sounds: /w/ + /r/. You can both try to do so if you want some comic relief. Now, hide the W with your finger and ask him to read it. This time, he should get it: RIST. Let him show you his WRIST.

Tell him, for reading purposes, WR = R. The W is "silent." You might appreciate how odd this must seem to a beginning reader. If a letter is silent, why use it in the first place? Worse yet, RIB, like WRIST, is a body part that starts with an R sound. Why isn't it spelled WRIB? (If he asks this question, see 3 possible answers above.) Happily, there are few words that start with the sound /r/ yet begin with W. Discuss with him the other 3 examples (for now) in the appendix.

Do KN as you did WR. KN can't be a blend because the sounds of these two letters don't flow together unless a vowel is placed between them. Show him the word KNOB on a card and tell him, once again, the first letter is silent. If necessary, hide the K with your finger. Once he reads it, use the word in a spoken sentence: "To open a door, turn its knob." So, for reading purposes, KN = N. Have him read the other 4 examples in the appendix. Let him know there are only a few words that have a silent K. (KNIFE, KNAVE, and other such words will show up when you cover long vowel sounds in Stage 11.) Compare the two words NOT and KNOT with him, making sure he understands the 2 different meanings. Point out that two of these 5 words (KNOB and KNOCK) involve doors.

The third and final example, WH, is a little more common than the other two – and in this case, it's the *second* letter, not the first that is silent. Place the following WH words on cards and have her try to read them:

WHEN   WHIP   WHIM

W and H can't be blended. To be consistent with what just happened above, she is likely to assume the first letter must be the silent one. If she does, she will read HEN, HIP, and HIM. Congratulate her on her clever decoding skills, but remind her she already knows (from earlier in this stage) how to spell HEN, HIP, and HIM. Explain that, in the case of WH, it's the *second* letter that is silent. Now ask her to try again. Hide the H if necessary and help with the meaning of WHIM. Have her read the rest of the WH words in the appendix. (You might point out that, for some reason, many of these WH words are great sound effects: WHAM! WHACK! WHUMP! WHAP!) So, for reading purposes, WH = W.

You've arrived at the point where your child knows a sound for every letter in the alphabet. Not only that, he can blend these sounds into hundreds of words – words he fully comprehends. Look at that stack of flash cards! To finish this stage, sum up all the anomalies for him. You might prepare 5 index cards as follows:

SIX   QUIT   WRIST   WHEN   KNOCK

On the back of each of these cards, write the incorrect, but phonetic spelling:

SIKS   KWIT   RIST   WEN   NOCK

Let him see the back of the card only if he needs help to pronounce the word.

As a final test before moving to Stage 8, pick 3-5 words from each of the 5 groups listed as "anomalies" in the appendix, write them on index cards, shuffle them, and see how he does. Stay with this topic until it is clear to you that he knows these 5 not-so-logical pronunciations.

Stage 8
The Sounds of CH, SH, TH
Forming the Plural

L et's take stock. The two of you have now examined all 26 letters of the alphabet. Those letters have provided a spelling for 23 of the 41 sounds listed in Table 1. (As you've seen, the letters C, Q and X only provide alternate spellings: C is an alternate spelling for /k/ or /s/, QU is an alternate for /k/ + /w/, and X for /k/ + /s/.) That leaves 18 sounds still to be studied, but no remaining single letters for symbolizing these sounds. So now the two of you are going to begin a new phase in your study of phonics. Since there are more sounds (41) in English than there are letters (26) to spell them, the remaining sounds will have to be symbolized by *pairs* of letters called *digraphs*. A digraph is a fancy name for a two-letter combination that spells a *single* sound. As such, a digraph is different from a blend.

Let's look at an example. In the word STOP, ST is a blend. Both sounds in the blend, /s/ and /t/, can clearly be heard when you say the word STOP. Now compare this word to SHOP. The SH in SHOP is not a blend, but a digraph. When you say this word, neither /s/ nor /h/ can be heard. Instead, you hear a new, single sound: /sh/. The sound /sh/ is one of the 41 elemental sounds of English listed in Table 1. To spell this sound, the digraph SH is used. Note that while STOP and SHOP both have 4 letters, SHOP has only 3 sounds:

$$STOP = /s/ + /t/ + /o/ + /p/ \quad \text{(ST is a blend)}$$
$$SHOP = /sh/ + /o/ + /p/ \quad \text{(SH is a digraph)}$$

You certainly won't need to get this detailed with your child. In fact, I don't want you to use the word "digraph" with him at all. Instead, I suggest you use the word **two-fer**, as in "two letters fer one sound." The main point you'll need to emphasize with your child is that two-fers are something new; they are not blends. Instead, they must be read as a two-letter unit that symbolizes a *single* sound.

In this stage, the two of you will encounter 3 important consonant digraphs: SH, CH, and TH. None of these digraphs (two-fers) are blends of the 2 letters that compose them. These 3 digraphs symbolize 3 brand-new sounds: /sh/, /ch/, and /th/. All of them are among the 41 unique, indivisible sounds of the English language listed in Table 1.

Start your child with the digraph SH. Ask him if he wants to learn a new sound. When he enthusiastically responds that he does, place your finger up to your lips and tell him SHHH! He'll look confused: was he being too loud? Explain to him the sound SHHH is precisely the new sound you want to cover. Tell him to listen for that same sound in the following words: SHIP, SHOP, SHOE, SHELF, SHOUT, SHORT, SHEET, SHARK, SHIVER, SHUT, BUSH, TRASH. Ask him to produce the sound himself. Once he gets it, ask him if it's sustainable. (This one is.)

The Spelling Corner: Spelling practice can now focus on all those new sounds represented by the letters H, J, V, W, Y, Qu, X and Z from Stage 7. Do the easy CVC words and consonant blends first. Stay with those words if she is finding the spelling difficult. If those words are easy for her, ask her to spell some of the words in the box labeled "Anomalies" in Appendix F. Caution her that you're going to ask for spellings of words with "silent" letters. In all cases, be sure to ask her to spell those 4 high-frequency words IS, HIS, AS, and HAS.

Present him with a dilemma: "How can we spell this sound if there are no letters left?" (Remind him he has already studied the sound of every letter in the alphabet.) If he suggests S, tell him that's the sound of a snake: SSSSS. Verbally contrast the two sounds /sh/ and /s/ – they are clearly different.

Discuss with him that one of the problems with English (there are many!) is that it has more sounds (41) than letters (26). So now we must start placing 2 letters together, as a unit, to spell a *single sound*. Tell him the SHHH sound (finger to lips again) is spelled SH (write it on paper and show it to him this time). Explain that SH is not a blend because the two sounds, /s/ and /h/, can't be blended. (The two of you can try, but it won't work!) Here is where you can tell him that since SH is not a blend, you're going to call it a **two-fer** because it's two letters fer one sound.

Review the 5 sounds of both S and H with him, and then ask if he can produce the 5 sounds of the two-fer SH: /sha/ /she/ (as in SHED) /shi/ /sho/ /shu/. Keep at it until he pronounces all 5 SH sounds correctly. Now write (on paper or your index cards) 5 words with the 5 SH sounds:

SHACK   SHED   SHIP   SHOP   SHUT

Can he read all five? Help if necessary by covering the *last* sound of these 5 CVC words with your finger. In the case of SHACK, this means covering CK. Note that I am still referring to these 5 words as CVC. Each of them consists in a single consonant sound, followed by a vowel, followed by another single consonant sound (CVC). You may also wish to discuss with him the following 3 words, which clearly show the difference between the sounds of S, H, and SH: SIP, HIP, and SHIP.

Once he knows the 5 sounds of SH and he can read the above 5 words, it is time to look at Appendix G. There you'll find about 50 SH words – a mix of simple CVC words and words which include the various blends we've already encountered. (I am no longer separating simple CVC words from consonant blends in the appendices.) Decide whether you want to transfer the words to flash cards (useful if you often need to hide letters with your finger) or whether you will have your child read the new words directly from the appendix.

Teacher Note: Here is an example of *faulty* instruction. Your child is having trouble reading the word SHACK so you hide the S and she reads the CVC word HACK. You then reveal the S. Your mistake? HACK has a clear H sound; SHACK has no H sound whatsoever. You separated a digraph. Digraphs like SH have a single sound. They can't be separated. Had the word been BLACK, separating the B from the L would be no problem. BL is a blend; SH is a digraph.

SQUISH is a difficult word. If necessary, replace the QU with KW (SKWISH) and hide the leading SK. Once he reads the CVC blend, WISH, uncover the K (KWISH), the S (SKWISH), and then rewrite the word as SQUISH, reminding him that, in English, the KW blend is always spelled QU.

Next, focus your child's attention on the digraph CH. This time, simply write CH on a piece of paper, show it to her, and tell her it's another example of a two-fer. The two of you can try to blend the sounds /k/ and /h/ – it won't work. Tell her CH spells another new sound and she should listen for it at the beginning of these words: CHIN, CHEST, potato CHIP, CHEW, CHILD, CHASE. This sound is also at the end of the words ITCH, SCRATCH, MUNCH, and RICH. It's at both ends of the word CHURCH. Stick with it until she can confidently pronounce the 5 sounds of CH: /cha/ /che/ /chi/ /cho/ (as in CHOP) /chu/ (as in CHUMP). Contrast these 5 sounds of CH with the 5 sounds of SH. Show her the words CAT, HAT, and CHAT – words which clearly show the difference between the sounds of C, H, and CH.

There are 4 different groupings involving CH in the appendix. Again, don't separate the C from the H when doing these with your child. If she is having trouble with the CVC word CHICK, for example, hide the CK with your finger, thus revealing only the CV part of the word. If she is having trouble with CHAMP, hide the P and show her the CVC word CHAM – then reveal the P. (Reminder: In this book, I don't use CVC to indicate consonant/vowel/consonant, but rather consonant sound/vowel sound/consonant sound. So, CHIMP is a CVCC word.)

Compare the two words WHICH and WITCH with your child, defining both, and acknowledging they have identical sounds but different spellings and meanings (thus they are homophones). Also point out that WHICH, like WHEN, is a question word, an *interrogative* – and both have a silent H. Post these two question words on a bulletin board where she'll see them often. You'll be adding about 8 more interrogatives as this reading program continues. All the interrogatives are important words.

The digraph TH is trickier than either SH or CH. If necessary, go back to Chapter 2 and review the fact that TH spells 2 different sounds: one voiceless, /th/, and the other voiced, /TH/. You'll explicitly teach your child the voiceless sound, although the appendix has *both*. Should you make this voiced/voiceless distinction with a beginning reader? I *would* make the distinction with an older child or with an adult learner, but I would not do so with a preschooler. A preschooler already uses the words THINK (voiceless) and THEM (voiced) without any trouble. Simply help with the correct pronunciation.

Tell your child you have one more two-fer. Write it out and show it to him: TH. Here are some words to introduce the (voiceless) sound: THIN, THICK, THUD, THINK, THING, THAW, THREE, THRILL, BATH, BOTH, WITH, EARTH, TOOTH. Once you're sure he can accurately produce the 5 sounds, /tha/ /the/ (as in THEFT) /thi/ /tho/ /thu/, compare and contrast the words TUG, HUG, and THUG. Then do the TH words in Appendix G. THRIFT is a tricky word (6 letters, 5 sounds). You can progressively do: RI (CV), RIF (CVC), RIFT, THRIFT if he has trouble. I have many words boxed as high-frequency words in the TH group. Note that most of these have the *voiced* TH sound.

Next: In Appendix G, you'll find two groups of rhyming words: the E/EE group and the ALL group. The E/EE group has over a dozen one-syllable words that end in either one or two E's. They all rhyme and they all have the long E sound: /E/. This sound is new for your child. What you have taught him up until now is "E says /e/." You may wonder why I want to deal with this group now, rather than wait until Stage 11 when I cover all the long vowel sounds. My reason is, in Stage 9, you'll have your child read lots of complete sentences. The E/EE group has numerous high-frequency words that will make the task of constructing decodable, full sentences much easier. In addition, this group is a stand-alone group in English. For most words ending in E, the E is silent. So this group can logically be covered almost any time. Finally, even the youngest new reader already knows the meaning of most of these words.

Don't present these words to your child the normal way, on flash cards. Since they rhyme and have the same structure (CV or CCV), present them *as a group*. Simply write them out on a piece of paper and show all of them to your child at once. Point out these are the first words he's seeing (so far) that *end* in a vowel. Tell him, for short words ending in E or double E, E does not say /e/, rather, E *says its own name*. Discuss this with him a little. This is his first hint that a single letter, in this case the letter E, can spell 2 different sounds: /e/ or /E/.

Read the first word for him: BE. Contrast it with BED. Can he hear the different sound of E in these two words? Use the word in a few spoken sentences: "Would you rather BE inside or outside today?" "BE quiet!" "Will you BE my friend?" Now, have your child read the second word (HE), reminding him that the whole group rhymes. Can he use it in a sentence?

As you continue down the list with him, talk about what it means for words to rhyme (same ending sound, but different beginning sound). Define any word he doesn't know and discuss the difference (in meaning) between BE and BEE. It should go quickly once he catches on. Tell him that if he forgets, and says these words with the wrong E sound, /e/, none of them are actual words! (Try it with him!) So, it's easy to remember this little group.

Let's talk about that tricky last word in the group: THE. It *could* be pronounced like all the rest of them, with a long E sound, but that's not the way most people pronounce this word in the United States. Most people pronounce it as /TH/ + /u/ (voiced TH plus short U). Your child has already said this word a million times; now he sees how to spell it. Simply acknowledge the slight sound difference. Write the following sentences on some paper and *ask him to do the reading*. The sentences highlight the E/EE group and they should be decodable for him. Nonetheless, take your time here. This reading of full sentences is new for him and it foreshadows what's coming next in Stage 9.

- THE bag is on THE shelf.
- Mom is on THE deck.
- THE man is in THE tub.
- Help ME with this job.
- Did HE help his dad?
- Will SHE sit with ME?
- WE SEE THE dog PEE on THE TREE.
- HE fell on his KNEE.

I would also present the ALL words from Appendix G as a group. I didn't include these words back in Stage 5 when the 2 of you studied the L sound because, in this group, A spells /aw/, not /a/. Think how the word BALL rhymes with CRAWL. Discuss with your child the fact that the A does indeed sound a little different in this group from what she is used to. Tell her what the first two words in the group say and allow her to read the rest of the group on her own, using the fact that all the words rhyme.

The last remaining topic in this stage is to examine what happens when we add an S to a word. We add an S for two reasons: first, to change a noun from singular to plural (BELL, BELLS) and second, to make a verb agree with its subject (I TELL, HE TELLS). The only complication is whether that final S keeps its S sound or takes on a Z sound. A handy rule is that if the original word ends in P, T, K, or F, an added S keeps its S sound (CAPS, ANTS, ROCKS, SURFS). In all other cases, the added S has a Z sound (BAGS, HOGS, NODS, BALLS, CANS, HAMS, JARS, COWS, PLAYS). Surprisingly, a final S says /z/ more often than it says /s/.

I don't think it's helpful to share this rule with a preschooler. Most children will pronounce the final S correctly without ever knowing the rule. If your child does have trouble with this, simply correct her pronunciation and tell her sometimes it just sounds better if a final S says /z/. In Appendix G, I have two groups of words ending in S: one group has the S sound, the other has the Z sound. Do them separately with your child, make flash cards, and then mix them together.

There is one complication I should mention here. If the original word ends in S, X, Z, CH or SH, you can't simply add an S. Instead, you must add ES, and the resulting new word has *two* syllables (KISSES, BOXES, FIZZES, PEACHES, DISHES). You'll cover this complication in Stage 10, after you introduce two-syllable words. For now, keep it simple as possible.

Stage 9
Reading Sentences (Part I)

During this stage, your child will advance to reading full, grammatically correct sentences. Don't worry about spelling practice; you can resume spelling again in Stage 10. Your goal here is to provide sentences that are within your child's ability to decode. In doing so, you'll be providing her with the opportunity to review all the sounds in the previous stages and, more importantly, you'll be enhancing her motivation and self-confidence.

At this point, you have exposed her to 27 of the 41 sounds of English: the 5 short vowel sounds (/a/ /e/ /i/ /o/ /u/) and 22 consonant sounds (/b/ /d/ /f/ /g/ /h/ /j/ /k/ /l/ /m/ /n/ /p/ /r/ /s/ /t/ /v/ /w/ /y/ /z/ /sh/ /ch/ /th/ and /TH/). Therefore, you must be careful about the sentences you ask her to read. The words in those sentences should have only the 27 sounds (and their spellings) she's already learned. There can be no two-syllable words or long vowel sounds for the simple reason that you have not yet formally taught those concepts. There can be no vowel two-fers (EA, OI, OU, and so on) for the same reason. In short, the sentences must be "decodable." I spoke of decodable text in Chapter 3, but I'll define it again here: text is *decodable* for a reader only if the reader has already been taught the skills necessary to do the decoding.

It is difficult to write full, decodable sentences with only 27 sounds at one's disposal. To make the task easier, I need you to teach her 12 of the 50 irregular words I first spoke of in Chapter 3. Being able to use these 12 irregular, high-frequency words will make the task of constructing decodable text much easier – both for me, and for you (should you decide to construct *additional* sentences). You'll teach the other 38 irregular words in Stages 12 and 15. Once your child masters these 12 words, she'll be ready to read the sentences later in this stage.

Tricky Words (12)					
you	do	her	they	my	to
who	our	their	your	have	from

Let me be specific about the criteria I used in writing the decodable sentences you'll find below. This should be helpful if you choose to make up some sentences on your own.

- All words should be one syllable.
- All vowels should have their short sound (exception: the E/EE words and the ALL words from Appendix G).

- Any word from the above Tricky Words (12) group is allowed.
- Interrogatives: when, which, who.
- Conjunctions: but, and.
- Any subject pronouns: I, you, he, she, it, we, they.
- Any object pronouns: me, you, him, her, us, them.
- Possessives: my, your, yours, his, her, hers, our, ours, their, theirs.
- Prepositions: to, in, with, on, at, from, off, up.
- Numbers: three, six, ten.
- Any word from Appendix A through Appendix G.
- Any word with an S added to form the plural, or to have a verb agree with the subject.

Before having your child tackle the decodable sentences that follow, she must easily and quickly recognize the above 12 tricky words (plus the words "I" and "a"). I'm not counting the words "I" and "a" among the tricky words because they're too trivial. You can dispense with these two familiar words right away.

Ask your child if she can name the two shortest words in our language. Whether she can name them or not, write them down and tell her how to say them. "I" says its own name and is always uppercase. It's the word we use when we speak about ourselves. Most children are already quite familiar with this word! In the word "a," the A does not say its own name; instead, it has the short U sound she already knows, /u/, and which is also present in the word THE. In fact, if pronounced as most people speak in the United States, the word "a" rhymes with "the." How weird is that? Tell her that's why it's tricky!

Next, tell her "a" or "an" usually come before a *noun*: a person, a place, or a thing – something we can touch. Write these examples on paper and allow her to read each one:

| a bag | a flag | an egg | a cat | a dog | a ball |
| an ox | a brick | a duck | a tree | an ant | a stick |

These nouns are all from earlier stages. Ask her if she can see why "an" is used sometimes instead of "a." If she can't, tell her "an" is used if the following noun starts with a vowel. It sounds better!

Now tell her "I" is usually followed by a *verb*: an action word. Write these examples:

| I swim | I fall | I yell | I run | I help | I see |
| I hug | I ask | I pee | I call | I slept | I jog |

Let her read each one and help as necessary. Tell her that by placing the word "I" in front of these verbs, we know exactly who is doing the action! Now have her read each of the following as you write them:

I swim	he swims
she swims	we swim
I yell	he yells
she yells	we yell

Emphasize that in each case, we know exactly who's doing the swimming and the yelling. Easy, right? Point out to her that a verb following SHE or HE usually has an S to make it sound better.

With the simple words "I" and "a" out of the way, focus next on the above 12 tricky words. Write each one on its own index card and spread them out in front of her. Explain why you call these words "tricky": the spelling and the sound don't quite match. Tell her all 12 are common words she uses all the time when she speaks. Can she recognize any of them? No? No problem.

Cover the E in HAVE with your finger and let her read it now. It has a silent E – no big deal. Write out a few sentences using HAVE on some paper and let her read them:

- We HAVE a cat.
- I HAVE a ball.
- I HAVE a rash on this leg.

You don't want her to blindly memorize these tricky words. Instead, you want her to use all the phonetic hints these words *do* possess. The word HAVE is on the tricky list simply because of the silent E. Tell her it ought to be spelled HAV. (No English words end in V.)

Take the HAVE card off the table and show her the card with HER on it. Does she recognize the word? Tell her the H and R sounds are exactly what they should be, but the E does not have the normal E sound: /e/. Nor does E say its own name (like in SHE). Write these sentences and let her read them. Can she decode this new word from context, knowing only the E is irregular?

- This is HER desk.
- HER name is Jan.
- I see HER red hat.
- HIS cat ran up the tree. (contrast HIS and HER as opposites)

When she knows the word, place it with the HAVE card. Ten cards to go.

The word FROM is almost perfectly phonetic. Again, only the vowel is a little off. Give him some sentences to read and he may get it without help:

- This frog is FROM the pond.
- That ball is FROM Dan.
- We ran FROM that big dog!

Tell him this word wouldn't be tricky at all if it were spelled FRUM. Acknowledge that strange spellings sometimes happen in English and retire the card.

Pick out the 4 cards with TO, DO, YOU, and WHO on them. Tell him these 4 words rhyme like the words HE, ME, BE, and SHE in Stage 8. Does he recognize them? Ask him to pronounce TO and DO using the short O sound, /o/, that he knows – and then the 2 of you can agree that no real word results from doing this. Let him know the word starting with W is a question word and let him attempt these sentences:

- WHO is that kid? That kid is Jack.
- WHO is tall? I am tall.
- WHO is small? Pam is small.
- WHO slept in this bed? Chuck did.

Compare the word WHO with the other 2 interrogatives he already knows:

- WHO is that kid? That kid is Rick.
- WHICH hat is his? The black hat is his.
- WHEN did she HAVE HER nap? She had HER nap at ten.

Point out that the H is silent in WHICH and WHEN, but in the tricky word WHO, the W is silent! In fact, WHO is tricky for 2 reasons: The W is silent and the O has an /ew/ sound, like in MOOSE. Now remind him the other three words rhyme with WHO. So, they must also have an /ew/ sound! Can he decode them now, based on their first letter? Use each in a simple sentence for him to read:

- Pass the cup TO me.
- Can YOU see me? I can see YOU.
- I can DO that job!
- DO YOU HAVE a dog? Yes, I DO.

Retire these 4 cards from the table. Five remain.

To introduce THEY to him, do what you were doing above, but this time with *all* the subject pronouns: I, you, he, she, it, we, they. Write this for him:

I swim.	You swim.	We swim.
He swims.	She swims.	They swim.

When he gets to the word THEY, does he recognize it? If not, tell him what the word is, and point out that the TH is perfectly phonetic (regular) but the EY is wacky. It's the EY that makes this a tricky word. Define it for him: WE means a group that includes me; THEY means a group that does not include me. These 6 important words tell us *who does the action.* Do the above with as many verbs as necessary (JOG, HUG, HELP, CALL, SEE, ASK) until he is comfortable with all 6 subject pronouns. Retire the THEY card.

The 4 remaining cards on the table are all possessives. These 4 words, along with HIS and HER, tell us *who the thing (noun) belongs to.* Write this for him:

his ball	her ball
my ball	your ball
our ball	their ball

These last 4 words are difficult, yet he must master them. Point out that YOUR is simply YOU with the R sound, /r/, at the end. For the word MY, at least the M sound is what we expect. For THEIR, the TH and the R sounds are fine; in fact, this word is pronounced like THEY, but with /r/ attached. The only phonetic sound in the word OUR is the final R. (OUR will turn out to be perfectly phonetic once you both study the OU two-fer in Stage 13.) Repeat the above exercise with lots of nouns until he is comfortable with all 6 possessives. Other nouns you might use are: DOG, HAT, FROG, BUG, TUB, SNACK, GIFT, and many more.

Don't let your child attempt to read the sentences below until he knows these 12 words thoroughly. He must simply recognize them, using all the phonetic hints they do have. Here is the final test of proficiency: mix these 15 index cards (the 12 tricky words plus "the," "I," and "a") and see if he can quickly recognize each word. He should be able to read all 15 words, in any order, in under a minute.

Suggestion: Post these 12 tricky words on a wall where your child will see them many times a day. Discuss them often. Is the E/EE group posted as well?

––

Assuming your child has mastered the above 12 tricky words, it's time for him to read some more sentences. Help only as needed, and only after giving him ample time on his own. This is a BIG step! These are full sentences that express a complete thought. Your child should be able both to decode them and to understand their meaning. As he decodes them over the next days (or weeks), use this opportunity to teach him some of the basic "mechanics" of sentences:

- Sentences always start with an uppercase letter.
- Sentences express a complete thought.
- Sentences end with a period, a question mark (?) or excitement mark (!).
- They use commas where there is a pause in the flow of speech.
- All sentences have a verb (an action word).
- Words in sentences are separated from each other by blank spaces.
- We always read from top to bottom and from left to right.
- The names of people start with an uppercase letter.

Don't expect your child to race through these sentences. As a beginner, he must take time to "sound out" (decode) the words based on his phonics skills from Stages 2-8. Have him read the sentences directly out of this book and check them off as he decodes them. Each day, have him review some of the sentences he has already decoded. If you find he simply can't read certain words, go back and review that particular stage. Don't let him skip words and don't allow guessing. Make sure he understands the meaning of the words he reads.

The two of you should take as much time as you need with these sentences; you need not adhere to anyone's schedule but your own. When you finish this stage, your child is a full-fledged reader by *any* standards. And this is true even though he knows only 27 of the 41 sounds in the English language. He's not yet fluent, but each day he will become more so. Sensing the magnitude of his own accomplishment and hearing your well-deserved praise, how can he not want to go on?

Decodable Sentences

I will sit with my mom.

We will swim in the pond.

You can sit with me.

They can sit in the grass.

He sits on the rug.

She stands on the wall!

I run with my small dog.

We ran up the hill to catch Jill.

You cant run with a cat! (proper contractions come in Stage 17)

They can run with us.

He went up the steps.

She jumps on the rug.

An egg is on my dish.

Is that an egg on your dish?

Their dog smells bad!

Our cat naps in the sun a lot!

Her glass has a crack in it!

His dog is a Pug.

Who is that lass? That lass is Jill. She is three.

Who is that lad? That lad is Sam. He is six.

Who is that tall man? He is my dad.

Which plant is his? The plant on the desk is his.

Which hat is hers? The hat in the red box is hers.

When will we have lunch? We will have lunch at three o'clock.   (help with o'clock as needed.)

When will she have her nap? She will have her nap at ten o'clock.

This is my pet frog. I call him Fred. He has bumps on his skin!

This is my cat. I call her Fluff. She sits on my lap.

Is this your glass of milk?
Yes, thats my glass of milk!   (proper contractions come in Stage 17)

We can smell the trash in the bin. It smells bad!

I had lunch with mom and dad at 11 o'clock.

Jack and Jill went up the hill to fetch their dog.

Did you have a snack? Yep, I had a snack with Kim.

Did you have a hot dog with your lunch? Yes. In fact, I had 2 of them – with ketchup!   (help with 'ketchup' as needed.)

My dog lifts his leg and then he pees on trees!

That frog jumps from the log into the pond.

I see you, but you cant see me!

Do you have my ball? Your ball is in the hall.

She sits on the rug. I will sit next to her.

We sat on a brick wall. Dan fell off and cut his leg!

That dog just bit me! I am sad and mad!

She has her red dress on and she fell in the mud!
Is her dress a mess?

The ants ran from the tree to their nest in the wall.

Who is that next to him? Thats his dad.

I will toss the ball to you. Hit it with your bat and then run fast!

A duck, on its back, quacks up!
Is that a jest? You quack me up!

A rich man has lots of cash to stash!

Will you help me lift this bench? I am glad to help you!

Thats a bug on your rug!

I wish I had a fish on my dish.

That duck is stuck in the muck, Chuck!

When I gulp my milk, Mom tells me to sip it.

You can jog with me, and then you can swim with them.

Help me get that cup. Its up on the top shelf.

He will be as tall as his dad.

Ed slept on a cot, but we slept in our bed. Our bed has a quilt on it.

If you grab a crab, it will pinch your hand!

You have a rash on your leg. It must itch a lot. Do you scratch it?

When I see my mom, I will kiss her! Then she will be glad.

Ben, when did your hen get free from its pen?

Do you see that lass who sits in the grass? She is my pal.

Sam spits in the grass. Yuck!

He yells when he gets mad.

When I pass gas, it smells bad!

Mom calls me to have lunch with her. Then she hugs me.

Its fun to sit on a branch in an elm tree!

A small hen is a chick.
A small dog is a pup.
A small bed is a crib.
A small lunch is a snack.
A big cup is a mug.

She went to the vet to pick up her sick dog.

Who is in the bath tub? Sam is in the bath tub. He is a mess! He fell in a ditch!

I splash in the bath with my red duck.

We went on a trip with my mom. We had such a blast!

Can you pick me up? Yes, I can – and I will not drop you.

Spell sad. Ok. S – A – D.
Spell mad. M – A – D.
Spell bad. B – A – D.
I am glad that you can spell this well!

A hen clucks. A duck quacks. A kid yells – and trash smells.

That big dish fell off the shelf by itself! I did not do it!

If you tell fibs, I cant trust you.

I help my mom: I dust the shelf and I mop the deck!

They went to the shop to get milk and snacks.

Fred and Ted fled on their red sled.

When will she call me? She will call you at ten o'clock.

Which kid hid my squid? Sid did. Sid hid your squid in that can with the lid.

Get your cup and I will fill it to the rim with pop.

Did she swim at camp? Yep, and then she slept in her tent!

It is rash to stash cash in the trash!

We will cuss and fuss if we miss that bus, Gus!

Which tree has a nest in it? That big elm tree on top of Moss Hill. The nest has three robins in it!

Stage 10
The Sound of NG and NK
Multi-Syllable Words

The next new sound you'll introduce to your child is spelled by another consonant two-fer: NG. Unlike the sounds of SH, CH, and TH, it's difficult to pronounce this new sound /ng/ in isolation from other sounds. You and your child have heard /ng/ hundreds of times because it occurs in such familiar words as SING, BANG, LONG and STUNG. However, if you try to pronounce the exact sound these 4 words have in common, you'll find it's an elusive sound.

You can avoid this difficulty with your child by attaching short vowel sounds to /ng/ right from the beginning. While /ng/, alone, may be difficult to hear and pronounce, /i/ + /ng/ = ING is easy. Therefore, you'll practice this sound with words having the spellings: ING, ANG, ENG, ONG, and UNG.

> **The Spelling Corner** – As a reminder: throughout this stage, you should practice spelling with words from Stage 8 (and Appendix G). These are the words with the digraphs SH, CH, and TH. Do the simple CVC words first and, whenever you can, build on the simpler word. For example, after he spells LUSH, ask about FLUSH and BLUSH; after ASH, ask him to spell SMASH, CRASH, and TRASH. Don't forget to include some words from the E/EE and the ALL groups.

Start with the ING sound, one of the more common sounds in the English language. Ask your child to say the word SING but without the initial S sound (don't write it yet). Help her out if necessary. This isolated ING sound, /i/ + /ng/, is what you want her to hear and to say. Now let her see how to spell this sound. Write ING on one of your index cards and show it to her. Have her repeat the sound. Point out that the I sound, /i/, can easily be heard, but the sounds, /n/ and /g/, are difficult to distinguish. That's because those two sounds *are not there*! NG (like SH, TH, and CH) is a two-fer. Just as SH is not a blend of /s/ + /h/, NG is not a blend of /n/ + /g/. NG spells a new sound.

> **Teacher Note**: The /ng/ sound is one of three nasal sounds in English. Take a moment to go back and look at the 41 sounds listed in Table 1. Note that you can pronounce any of these sounds perfectly well with your nose pinched shut *except* for /m/, /n/, and /ng/. These 3 sounds require air to be exiting the nose. You and your child can have some fun trying to say various NG words in this stage with your nose pinched shut.

Once she is comfortable with the ING sound, write an S in front of the ING on your index card. She should now recognize it as the word SING. Write RING and WING below SING and have her read those as well.

SING
RING
WING

Now add a B to the word RING and an S to the word WING and let her decode those too. Show her the entire list of ING words in Appendix H and see how she does. At the end of that list is a review of important subject pronouns and possessives.

The next day, review ING with him and write ANG on an index card. Can he pronounce it correctly? He need only take the sound of ING and replace the initial /i/ with /a/. If necessary, have him say the word BANG but without the B sound. Have him compare the spelling and the sound of both ING and ANG. When he seems comfortable with ANG, have him read the 9 ANG words in the appendix. It would also be helpful to mix the ING and ANG words together, and see how he does.

With ING and ANG fresh in his mind, write UNG on some paper and ask him to pronounce it. Tell him to take his pronunciation of either ING or ANG and change the initial sound to /u/. There are 8 UNG words in the appendix.

Similarly, do ONG and ENG with your child. There are no English words of consequence that *end* in ENG. I suggest you write ENG on an index card, get the correct sound, and then add the two-fer TH at the end: ENGTH. Once she has that sound, the two words LENGTH and STRENGTH from the appendix should become decodable for her. These two words are phonetic but they are difficult at first. Once you finish the NG groups, have her tell you the 5 sounds of NG: ANG, ENG, ING, ONG, UNG. Then let her read some new sentences:

Our king is a strong man.

I sang a song with my mom.

That bee stung my leg!

Who rang that bell?

If you step in dung, you will be sad.

Of course, you can make up your own sentences for your child whenever you wish. Just be sure to stick to the criteria listed in Stage 9 plus any new words and sounds you are working on here in Stage 10. You don't want to confuse her with text you have not yet taught her to decode.

The NK groups in Appendix H are next. Before you discuss this topic with your child, note that NK is something of an anomaly in English. It does not spell a unique sound like NG, but neither is it a normal blend. Most blends simply combine the sounds of their component letters. For example, SP = /s/ + /p/. But NK is not a combination of /n/ + /k/. Instead, NK = /ng/ + /k/. Consider the word THINK. You don't say THIN and add a K sound; you say THING and add the K sound. In other words, THINK = THING + /k/. Using our notation:

THING = /th/ + /i/ + /ng/   while   THINK = /th/ + /i/ + /ng/ + /k/

Here are other examples:

RANK = RANG + /k/   KINK = KING + /k/
DUNK = DUNG + /k/   CLINK = CLING + /k/

The question is, how shall you present all of this to your child? I suggest you place the word STINK on an index card and ask her to read it. She'll probably have some difficulty because NK is not a reasonable consonant blend in English. The sounds /n/ and /k/ do not easily flow together. After discussing this with her, write the following under the word STINK:

STINK
STINK = STING + K

If necessary, explain the meaning of the symbols = and +. Tell her to say this new word by saying STING and immediately adding the K sound: /k/. Does she get it? Here are other word pairs you can do with her in the same manner:

WING/WINK   SING/SINK
BRING/BRINK   BANG/BANK
SANG/SANK   FLUNG/FLUNK

She'll probably find this pretty interesting. You want her to learn that, when reading, she should always handle NK in the following manner: (show this to her)

ANK = ANG + K
INK = ING + K
ONK = ONG + K
UNK = UNG + K

Help her to compare the 5 sounds of NG (ANG, ENG, ING, ONG, UNG) with the 5 sounds of NK (ANK, ENK, INK, ONK, UNK). Now go to Appendix H and let her read the 4 groups of NK words she'll find there. (There are no ENK words in English.) When you finish the NK groups, mix up some NG and NK flash cards and make sure she can read them competently.

Before moving on to Stage 11, there are a few more topics to address. Your child needs to understand that not all words are short, one-syllable words. To that end, you'll need to define *syllable* in a way he can understand. Then you can give him some practice in decoding some two-syllable words on his own.

The number of syllables is different from the number of sounds. The word CAT has 3 sounds but it's a single syllable – a single pulse of sound. The word CHILLY has 6 letters, 4 sounds (/ch/, /i/, /l/, /E/) and 2 syllables (CHIL, LY). The problem here, is how to explain "syllable" to your child. My Merriam-Webster dictionary states that a syllable is "a unit of pronunciation having one vowel sound, with or without surrounding consonants, forming the whole or a part of a word." I like this definition – but not for a child.

I suggest a different approach. Point out to him that most of the words he has looked at so far (the words in Appendices A to G) have only 2 to 5 letters each – they are small words. Tell him it's time to look at some bigger words – words that have two parts. That should get his attention! Sit down with him at a table, take some paper, and write the following word with the letters spread out a little bit:

P U M P K I N   (Don't let him see what you are writing)

Now use a blank index card (you've got lots of those!) and cover KIN. Ask him to read what he can see: PUMP. Tell him: "PUMP is only the first part of this word – now here is the second part." Slide the index card over to cover PUMP and again ask him to read. He should say KIN. Now take the card away and ask him to read the whole word rapidly. This word is likely in his vocabulary and he should now recognize it: PUMPKIN. Reiterate that this word has two "parts" and point out that each "part" has its own vowel. These "parts" are called "syllables." So, define "syllable" for him in one (or both) of these ways:

- *syllable* - the number of "parts" in a word (each part has a vowel)
- *syllable* - the number of sounds you hear if you mumble the word with your mouth closed, as though you are humming. Try it!

He should be eager to do this again. Continue the game with these (or other) words from Appendix H, covering one part and then the other. Each time he gets the word, point out that each syllable (or part) has its own vowel:

VAN / ISH
BAS / KET
CON / TEST

C H I C / K E N
I N / S E C T

Ask him if he would like to try some *three*-part words: (Who could say no?)

F A N / T A S / T I C
P U N / I S H / M E N T
D I F / F I / C U L T
E X / P E C / T E D
A S / T O N / I S H

The multi-syllable words in Appendix H use only the 28 sounds your child already knows. Many are words he will recognize once he decodes them.

You shouldn't need to present every multi-syllable word in Appendix H as you did above, covering parts of each word with an index card. Once he catches on to this new idea of words having more than a single syllable, test how he does simply reading the entire word, written normally, on a flash card. Nor is it necessary to do all the multi-syllable words in Appendix H. You're already at the point where your child can read far more words than you can list. (Think about how amazing that fact is!) Simply pick 20-30 words from Appendix H that you know are in his vocabulary and put those words on flash cards. Help as needed and teach some new vocabulary. Note: future word lists will now routinely have some multi-syllable words included.

Now that your child is familiar with two-syllable words, you can finish up what you began in Stage 8. Back there, I said if a word ends in S, X, Z, CH, or SH, forming the plural can't be done by simply adding an S. Instead, you must add ES. This creates a second syllable where the final S always has a Z sound. There is a group of such words in Appendix H. I don't think it will require much time to do these with your child.

Your child can add his newly-learned suffix, ING, to many of the words in Appendices A through G. There is a simple rule governing the spelling:

- If a single consonant follows the vowel, double it and add ING (WIN, WINNING)
- If 2 consonants follow the vowel, just add ING (MELT, MELTING)

There are some words in Appendix H that show both of these situations. You and your child can examine these words together.

Stage 11
Long Vowel Sounds

Now it's time for your child to focus on the 5 long vowel sounds. Learning which spellings can symbolize these new sounds will enable her to read thousands of additional words. These five long vowel sounds, only four of which are unique, plus the 28 sounds already covered, will bring her total to 32. You'll recall from Table 1 that the English language has 41 sounds.

The Spelling Corner – The words you spell with your child during this stage can now come from Stage 10. Start with the simplest one-syllable NG and NK words. If those get easy for her, move on to some two-syllable words. Remind her each syllable must have a vowel. Start with the easier ones (EXIT, SUNSET, SICKNESS, CONTEST) and then move to the words having double consonants in the middle (HAPPEN, MUFFIN, SWIMMING). Remind her that when adding ING to a word having only a single consonant after the vowel, she must double the consonant.

As you begin Stage 11, review with your child what the vowels are and why they are the most important letters: every word and every syllable must have one. Point out that all the two and three-syllable words recently studied in Stage 10 had a vowel in each syllable. Tell her *another* reason vowels are so important is that each vowel can spell a second sound! Consonants, with a few exceptions, can't do this. This complicates things a little. Up until this moment, you have given her the impression that each vowel makes a single sound, so this new revelation may cause some confusion for a while. Briefly review with her the short vowel sounds she already knows: /a/ /e/ /i/ /o/ /u/.

So, what is the other sound a vowel can make? Tell her the vowel can sometimes say its own name: A, E, I, O, U. (/A/, /E/, /I/, /O/, /y/ + /ew/.) You might remind her that she has already seen this occur in the E/EE group back in Stage 8: ME, BE, SHE, TREE, and so on. Start with this example: Write the word TAP on an index card and let her read it. Now ask her to think of the word TAPE. She knows what TAPE is; she has probably used it in arts and crafts many times. Ask her what letter the word TAPE should start with, given its initial sound. She'll probably answer T. Write a second T under the T of the word TAP on your index card. Now ask her what letter the word TAPE should end with, given its final sound. She'll answer P. Write a second P under the P of the word TAP. Now ask her what vowel she can clearly hear in the middle of the word TAPE: A. Write that letter as well. Your index card now looks like this:

T A P
T A P

Ask her what she thinks. Does she see the problem? How can we have the same spelling for the words TAP and TAPE? Emphasize that for one of these two words (the top one), the A says what it has always said up until now: /a/. But in the second word, A says its own name: /A/. The problem is, how can we tell them apart? If A can make 2 different sounds, how do we know when A says /a/ and when A says /A/? Having set up this dilemma, you can now show her the solution. Write an E at the end of the second word:

T A P
T A P E

Problem solved! Tell her the E makes no sound but it lets her know that the earlier (preceding) vowel says its own name. The silent E is a signal to her; it tells her A says its own name, /A/, rather than /a/.

She is likely to find this confusing for a while, so you can do another example, this time ending up with:

P I N
P I N E

Tell her the sounds /a/, /e/, /i/, /o/, and /u/ are called **short** vowel sounds, while /A/, /E/, /I/, /O/, and /y/+/ew/ are called **long** vowel sounds.

> **Teacher Note**: I am using the correct notation with you. It's not for your child. When dealing with her, simply say what the long and short vowels sounds are.

The long sound of a vowel is precisely the *name* of that vowel. Explain that the words "short" and "long" have nothing to do with duration of the sound – they are simply traditional terms, used by teachers since just after the Big Bang.

Now ask him: What *two* sounds does A make? The verbal answer you want, of course, is /a/ and /A/. Write MAD and MADE on a card and ask which A is long and which is short. Can he read the two words? Ask him for the 2 sounds of the other 4 vowels as well. Next, get out a sheet of paper and write these two columns of words:

CAP	CAPE
PET	PETE
FIN	FINE
NOT	NOTE
CUB	CUBE

Discuss these two columns with your child. Help him pronounce the second column as needed. You want him to see how the silent E (an unpronounced E) changes both the sound and the meaning of the word, like magic! Point out how easy the long vowel sound is: the vowel says its own name! Make sure he understands the meaning of all 10 words.

To test his understanding of this important new concept, write out the following words in a *single* column on some paper:

win	hat	man	glob	van	scrap	mop
rip	cod	grim	cut	rod	cop	slop
Jan	bit	kit	spit	shin	mad	glad
fat	mat	pan	hid	dim	spin	fad
quit	Tim	gal	strip	snack	back	lick

Now, one at a time, go back up to the top of your column and, across from the word WIN, write WINE. Can he read both WIN and WINE correctly without help from you? Continue down the column, writing the same word, but now attaching an E. Each time, let him read both words. Your paper will look like this:

win	wine
hat	hate
man	mane
glob	globe
van	vane (and so on...)

Take 1 day or 5 days to do this; it doesn't matter. Discuss how fabulous this short and long vowel stuff really is. You might also discuss with him that this is not his first example of a "silent" letter: in WHEN, the H is silent; in WRECK, the W is silent. Even though the final E is silent, *it plays a key role*: it's a signal to the reader that the earlier vowel should say its long sound instead of its short sound. <u>Note</u>: for the final 3 words in the box above, drop the C when you add the E.

Now take a look at Appendix J. There, I have grouped words by long vowel, and, within each group, I have placed rhyming subgroups. Once your child has caught on to the fact that a silent E makes the earlier vowel "long," he may be able to read these new words quite rapidly. You may need to spend more time here on the meaning of words rather than on their decoding.

Teacher Note: A word about flash cards. You might judge it unnecessary here to make any flash cards at all. Your child might be able to simply look at Appendix J with you and read most of the words in the rhyming groups. Use your judgment going forward and use flash cards only when you think they will help. If you do use them, you can no longer hide any of the letters with your finger. Your child now needs to see the entire word at once to read it properly.

The long E group has fewer words than the others. That's because long E is usually spelled in a different manner, something you'll discuss with your child further below.

Also, a word about the long U sound. Sometimes, like the other long vowels, U says its own name: /y/ + /ew/:

CUBE = /k/ + /y/ + /ew/ + /b/
MUTE = /m/ + /y/ + /ew/ + /t/

At other times, however, that subtle /y/ sound is missing:

PRUNE =/ p/ + /r/ + /ew/ + /n/
FLUTE = /f/ + /l/ + /ew/ + /t/

You'll cover the latter case in Stage 13 when you look at the various spellings of the sound /ew/. Either way, however, long U is *not* a unique sound in English. It is always equivalent to /y/ + /ew/ or to /ew/ alone. (This discussion of long U is only for you; you need not bring it to your child's attention.)

The word USE in the long U group merits some special attention. It can be pronounced with the S symbolizing either /s/ or /z/. It makes a difference with the word's meaning. You can USE the following sentences to demonstrate the difference to your child. Just speak them; they are not yet decodable for him:

We USE a brush to clean our teeth.

versus

What's the USE of talking to that dog? He never listens!

A good test of Appendix J mastery is to take 2 words from each rhyming group and put them on flash cards. Mix up the cards and see if he can read them competently. You don't want to be in the position where your child needs rhyming to read well.

Next, the 2 of you will investigate another way English spells long vowels. So far, you and your child have encountered no *vowel* two-fers, that is, two consecutive vowels making a single sound. You'll begin to look at this situation now because there are four vowel two-fers that usually spell a long vowel sound. Here they are:

AI spells /A/   example: TRAIL
EA and EE spell /E/   examples: CHEAT, STREET
OA spells /O/   example: BOAT

> **Teacher Note**: When discussing these new vowel digraphs with your child, keep using the term "two-fer" rather than "digraph," as you did in Stage 8 with the consonant digraphs SH, CH, and TH. The essence of a two-fer is two letters fer one sound.

When the above 4 vowel combinations occur, *the first vowel is long and the second is silent.* You can see many more examples if you check out Appendix K. You can describe this situation to your child as follows: "When two vowels go walking, the first does the talking." This traditional rule is useful because your child will likely remember it due to the rhyme. In Appendix K, you can see how many common and important words have "two vowels walking." The danger with this rule is that a child may try to apply it to other vowel digraphs, where it doesn't work at all: OO, OI, AU, OU for instance. More about this later.

As your child decodes the words in Appendix K, do them in the order indicated: long O words, then long E, and finally, long A. I say this because the word OATMEAL, for instance, in the long E group presupposes the word OAT from the long O group.

You and your child should pay close attention to the 16 words in the appendix that I have marked as "EA exceptions." Most of them are familiar words and they clearly do not obey the "two vowels walking" rule. It's safe to say that every rule one might think of has exceptions when pronouncing English words. Nevertheless, some are worth mentioning, like this "two vowels go walking" rule, because they can help beginners, despite the inevitable exceptions. In the material ahead, I'll mention some other rules as well. In each case, I'll list the most common exceptions.

Once again, you face the question of whether to use flash cards or to simply have your child read directly from the lists in the appendix. In any case, the test for mastery here is the same as above: place 7-10 words from each of the four groups (OA, EA, EE, and AI) on flash cards and mix them up. Can he read the words competently when they are mixed?

I recommend you *do* place the 16 EA exceptions from the appendix on flash cards and discuss them with your child. Note that for eight of these exceptions, the correct way to pronounce the word is to let the *second* vowel "do the talking." The other eight are pronounced as if the A were not there. Note, too, I have reproduced the E/EE group from Appendix G to Appendix K where it more naturally belongs.

To finish this stage, you and your child can practice adding S (or ES) and ING to some of these new long vowel words. There is a small section for each of these tasks in Appendix K. The only *new* wrinkle is this: if a word ends in a silent E, drop the E before adding ING.

Stage 12
Reading Sentences (Part II)

L et's return to reading full sentences. These decodable sentences will be more complex than those your child looked at in Stage 9 because they now include all the material from Stages 10 and 11, as well as some new, tricky words. Here are the criteria I used for constructing these new sentences:

- All the previous criteria from Stage 9 *plus* the following:
- Two syllable words are now ok.
- All the words on the Tricky Words (31) list below.
- The /ng/ sound and the NK blend from Stage 10.
- All the long vowel sounds and their spellings from Stage 11.
- Present, past, and future conjugations of the irregular, but common verbs: to be, to do, to say, to go, to come, to have, to give. Also, the perfect and progressive forms of these verbs.
- New interrogatives: what, where.
- New numbers: one, five, seven, nine, eleven, twelve, fifteen, sixteen, seventeen, nineteen, one hundred.
- New preposition: of.
- New conjunction: because.
- Suffixes: S, ES, ING, FUL, MENT, LESS, NESS.

This is a lot of new material for sentence construction! As you can see, the following Tricky Word list repeats the 12 words from Stage 9, so there are "only" 19 new words here. They are all important for fluent reading.

Tricky Words (31)					
you	do	her	they	my	to
who	our	their	your	have	from
are	was	were	say	says	said
go	goes	come	give	what	where
one	of	been	does	gone	because
		done			

Your first goal in this stage is to help your child learn the above 19 new tricky words. (This could take awhile.) As you did in Stage 9, write them on individual flash cards and spread them out on a table in front of your child. Tell him that, except for the 2 words that start with O (OF and ONE), the *first* letter in each word is perfectly regular, meaning, it provides the correct first sound for the word. Also, he uses these words every day and knows each one of them in speech. Can he recognize any of them?

Pick out these 6 cards: GIVE, DONE, GONE, COME, ARE, and WERE. Now cover the ending E with your finger and he may be able to identify some of them. Remind him that, normally, the silent E would make the prior vowel long. But these are tricky words – so *none* of these vowels will have their long sound! Write some sentences for him to read and maybe he can figure out what the word is in context:

- GIVE me a drink.
- Will you GIVE me a hand with this job?
- Have you DONE your job yet?
- Is she DONE with her bath?
- They have all GONE to the game.
- The cake is GONE! Who ate it?
- COME here you rascal!
- Will you COME home with me?
- The kids ARE running in the grass.   (action is occurring now)
- The kids WERE running in the grass.   (action already occurred)

Make the following points with him as he reads the above sentences:

- GIVE should rhyme with FIVE and DIVE, right? But it doesn't. Given its actual pronunciation, it ought to be spelled GIV, but it isn't. That's why it's on the Tricky Word list!
- DONE should rhyme with BONE and CONE. Given the way we pronounce it, *ask him* how DONE should be spelled: DUN.
- Given their spelling, DONE and GONE should rhyme, but they don't. Don't ask him how GONE should be spelled – we haven't yet discussed one of its sounds: GONE = /g/ + /aw/ + /n/.
- COME should rhyme with HOME or it should be spelled CUM. Because it does neither, it's a tricky word!
- ARE is pronounced the same as the name of the letter R.
- WERE rhymes with an earlier tricky word: HER.

Set these 6 words to the side – 13 more to go!

Next, separate out the 3 cards with the words DOES, WAS, and BECAUSE. Make the point that these words should not rhyme, but, despite their weird spellings, they do! That's what makes them tricky! Does she recognize any of them? The word DOES is related to the tricky word DO from Stage 9. Have her focus on the first 5 sentences, below, and help her correct the third one, if needed. Once she knows how to pronounce DOES, ask her how it ought to be spelled: DUZ. Let her read the other sentences involving DOES.

Now, remind her that the other two words rhyme with DOES. Using that information, can she read the final two sentences? Help as needed. How should these words be spelled? (WUZ and BECUZ.)

- I do my job.
- We do our job.
- She do her job. → She DOES her job.
- You have a big dog. DOES he bite?
- DOES a chicken have lips? DOES a snake have hips? I think not!
- Mom WAS glad to see me. She gave me a big hug and kiss.
- I need a bath BECAUSE I fell in the mud.

Set these 3 cards off to the side with the other six – ten to go.

Tell him there are 2 more question words in front of him that belong with the 3 he already knows (WHEN, WHICH, and WHO), and that they, too, start with W. Allow him to pick out the WHAT and WHERE cards. Can he figure out what these two words are in the context of some sentences?

- WHAT is your name? My name is Kate.
- WHAT time is it? It's five o'clock.
- WHERE is my dog? I need to feed that mutt!
- WHERE is my hat? It's beginning to rain!

Discuss how these new question words would be spelled if they were better behaved: WUT and WARE (or WAIR). Two more cards off to the side; eight to go.

BEEN would be perfectly phonetic if the reader were British, but in the States, most people pronounce this word in a slightly different manner: BIN. See if your child can recognize this word in the following sentences:

- WHERE have you BEEN? I need your help.
- You rascal! Have you BEEN hiding from me?
- It has BEEN quite hot! WHERE is my fan?

Do the words ONE and OF together. These are two (of the three) most outrageous, non-phonetic, yet common words in the English language! (You'll cover EYE later.) Make fun of how these 2 words are spelled and he'll remember them forever. Despite the ridiculous spellings, let him try these sentences:

- ONE of my socks is missing!
- ONE cupcake plus ONE cupcake is 2 cupcakes!

- Do you think OF me when I am GONE?
- I think OF you all the time BECAUSE I like you!
- ONE OF my best pals is Dave.

How *should* these wacky words be spelled? Let him try: WUN and UV! Three more cards (OF, ONE, and BEEN) off to the side – five to go.

GO and GOES both involve motion, so do these together. Tell him that unfortunately, GO does not rhyme with TO, DO, and WHO from the tricky word list in Stage 9. Does he know what this word is? Simply tell him the O is long.

- I GO home.
- You GO home.
- She GO home.   →   She GOES home.
- They GOES home.   →   They GO home.
- WHERE did she GO?   I need to speak with her.
- I hope I can GO with you!
- He GOES to sleep at ten o'clock.
- She GOES shopping when she needs bread.

How should GOES be spelled in order for it to be phonetic? GOZE. Three tricky words remain.

These last 3 words, SAY, SAYS, and SAID are certainly related. Tell your child all of them involve people speaking. Try these sentences on him:

- I SAY: go to bed!
- You SAY: go to bed!
- She SAY: go to bed   →   She SAYS: go to bed!
- WHAT did you just SAY? I SAID I do not need a nap!
- Can you GO with me? Yes, my dad SAYS that I can!
- She SAID I broke the glass, but Mike did it, not me!
- Dad SAYS he will GO with me.
- Mom SAYS I can have an extra cupcake to take along with me.

SAY is spelled exactly as it should be spelled, and it will become perfectly phonetic in Stage 14. SAYS and SAID, on the other hand, should be spelled SEZ and SED.

Before proceeding to the new decodable sentences, take whatever time is necessary to make sure your child has mastered all 31 of the above tricky words. They are among the most frequently-used words in the English language. Shuffle the flash cards containing these words and practice with her until she knows them cold. If she has trouble with a given word, point out all the phonetic hints that might help her. When you are sure she is ready, continue on to the following sentences.

With the 31 irregular words out of the way, it's time for your child to tackle some new sentences. As before, give her ample time to read each sentence on her own. There is one new feature in these sentences that was not present in the earlier ones: quotation marks. Simply explain the use of these to your child as they come up. Again, no guessing or skipping over words. Make sure she understands whatever she reads. Have fun!

Decodable Sentences

to be

I am in the kitchen.

We are in the kitchen.

You are at the lake.

They were on the bus.

He is from Spain.

She is from Canada.

I was brushing my hair.

We were at the picnic.

She was on a hike.

He was with his mom at the fair.

Where have you been? I have been riding my bike.

to go

I go to the dentist.

We go to the ball game.

She goes to sleep at nine o'clock.

He goes to jail! Yikes!

They went up the stairs.

She went to get a bath.

Are you going to eat lunch with me?

Where have they gone? They have gone fishing at the lake.

to give

Can you give me a hand? Yes, I am glad to help you.

Did you give a dime to Ted? I gave Ted five dimes!

Will you give me a ride to the picnic?

Rain gives me a chill!

That bug gives me the creeps!

He is giving his dad help cleaning the kitchen.

Has she given you a reason for being this late?

to come

They come from the state of Texas. He comes from Alabama.

He came into the kitchen to eat salad and roast beef.

Where did you come from? I just came from the basement.

He comes home on his bike.

She is coming home with her skates.

to say

I say you are cheating! Well, I say you are quite wrong to think that of me!

What did they say? They said they are going to the beach.

He says he is feeling ill.

She says its time to eat lunch.   (proper contractions in Stage 17)

He says he will not go with me.

Mike said: "I think I will have a cup of tea, toast, and an egg."

to do

Who do you think you are?

Does a fish ride a bike? Does a hen take a hike?

Do you dream when you sleep? Do you moan when you weep?

Did the boat float, or did it sink?

What have you done? I have made a cake!

Gail, you look pale. Did you see a whale?

What is your name? My name is Steve.

Will you teach me to read? Thats what I am doing, pal!

Thank you! You are welcome!

I have been in the kitchen baking bread with mom.

One thing I like to do is to eat a fine meal.
Do you mean mac and cheese?
Yes! That meal cant be beat!

I must be getting sick. I keep sneezing and snot keeps dripping from my nose! Yuck!

I just got a drink at the kitchen sink.

Where is our dog? I have a big bone to give him!

If you mix red paint with white paint, you will get pink paint.

That junk in the trunk stinks. What is all that stuff?

I went home because it was late.

The boat sank because it hit a rock. The rock made a hole in the bottom of the boat.

Does the rain in Spain fall on the plain, Jane?

The sailboat at the dock was rocking in the breeze as the tide came in.

"What is she drinking?" said Ted.
"She is drinking tea with lemon," said Linda.

Mom! The mailman is here. He says he needs to speak with you.

I hear the train as it travels along the railroad track.

Does he wish to go swimming with us?
Yes, he does. He likes to swim.

I smile when I am glad. I yell when I am mad. I hide when I am bad. I sob when I am sad.

The king and the queen, sitting on their thrones, drank wine and ate roast chicken at their wedding feast.

I must clean the kitchen. Can you give me a hand?
Yes, I will help you.

Where have you been?
I have been shopping. I have cake, bananas, and pretzels to share with you. Yum!

Are you done with that cake? If you are, I will finish eating it. I hate to see it go to waste!

"Eat your ham and egg sandwich and drink that milk," said mom. "Then you will get big and strong."

Where is my jump rope? Did you take it?

What are you wearing on your head? These are earmuffs!

What do you like to eat?
I like pancakes and tea when I wake up – and mac and cheese with a hot dog at lunch time!

Stop all that groaning and moaning! You made that mess. Cleaning it up will not take you long at all!

We saw a cricket, a frog, a rabbit, and a snake in the grass!

What reason do you have for yelling? Are you in pain?

A cut-up peach on top of hot oatmeal, with cream, is a great breakfast!

Stop tipping that chair back! You will fall on your head and crack your skull!

"Gimme more cake!" said James. "Did you mean to say, 'Can I have more cake, please?' " said mom.

Can I please taste your wine, dad?
Yes, in sixteen years you can taste my wine!

Brush your teeth before you go to bed, ok?
All of them?
Yes please, dear.

The chain came off my bike while I was riding! Will you help me fix it?

I like pears, apples, and bananas – but not grapes!

Where is Kim?
She is sitting in the shade near that pine tree.

"Dad, where do children come from?" said Sam.
"It beats me," said Dad, "Go ask your mom. Perhaps she can explain it."

Keep that gate shut! If you do not, my dog will escape.

When I inhale, I fill my lungs with fresh air!

A bee stung me three times on my knee! Thats bad luck!

Toss the ball to me again! This time I will catch it!

"Time to get a bath," said mom. "You are not going to bed until you are clean."
"A bath! You must be joking!" said Melvin. "I just had one last week! Must I use soap? Can it wait until next month?"

(Some optional math follows. The word MINUS has a long I.)

This is math:

If you add three dimes to six dimes, you will have nine dimes.

Three plus six is nine (3 + 6 = 9)
Nine minus three is six (9 − 3 = 6)
Nine minus six is three (9 − 6 = 3)
One plus six is seven (1 + 6 = 7)
Seven minus one is six (7 − 1 = 6)
Seven minus six is one (7 − 6 = 1)
Three plus seven is ten (3 + 7 = 10)
Ten minus three is seven (10 − 3 = 7)
Eleven minus five is six (11 − 5 = 6)
Five plus six is eleven (5 + 6 = 11)
Ten plus six is sixteen (10 + 6 = 16)
One plus three plus five plus six is fifteen
(1 + 3 + 5 + 6 = 15)

+ means "plus" or "add"
− means "minus" or "subtract"
= means "is"

Gosh! I think I like this math stuff!

Stage 13
Other Vowel Sounds

So far, you've covered 32 of the 41 sounds in the English language. In this stage, you'll teach 8 more to your child, all of them vowel sounds, and all of them spelled with various two-fers. You can hear these 8 new sounds in the following words:

/ew/	stew, moon, glue
/oo/	good, took, could
/oy/	toy, coin
/ow/	cow, out
/aw/	law, fraud
/ar/	car, park, are
/er/	her, bird, turn
/or/	store, north

Notice that all these sounds are different from both short vowel and long vowel sounds. They are unique; all of them are included in the 41 elemental sounds of English listed in Table 1. You can also see there are multiple spellings for each of these sounds.

The Spelling Corner – Pick words from Stage 11 to spell with your child. Ask for the spelling of words from Appendix J for a few days. These are words where the vowel is long due to a silent E at the end of the word. Then switch to words from Appendix K where vowels are long due to "two vowels walking." As he gets good, alternate between the two appendices.

Be on the look-out for "good" mistakes. For example, you ask him to spell the word CAME and he answers K-A-I-M. This is a good mistake because, phonetically, he's correct. AIM and MAIM are both spelled similarly. It shows great understanding, but in practice, it's still wrong. He chose the wrong way to spell /A/ and he chose the wrong letter to symbolize /k/. Congratulate him for his ingenuity, but correct his spelling.

Look at Appendix L where I have words categorized according to these final 8 vowel sounds. Note, first, I have listed 4 different spellings for the sound /ew/: OO, EW, UE, and U-E. Examples using these spellings are ZOO, CHEW, BLUE, and JUNE. Your child has already seen multiple spellings, particularly for some of the long vowel sounds. Long A, for instance, can be spelled by attaching a silent E (GAME) or by combining A with I (RAIN). The sound /ew/, however, is in a class by itself. Take a moment and look it up in Appendix P. There you'll find a total of 10 spellings for this one sound!

A judgment call is needed here between two competing values: being complete, but avoiding needless complexity for the beginning reader. Here is what I have done in this case. I cover the four most important spellings of /ew/ in Appendix L. You saw the O spelling (TO, DO, WHO) and the OU spelling (YOU, YOUR) in the Tricky Word list back in Stage 9. No other common words have the O spelling, and the only other common words with the OU spelling are GROUP, SOUP, and YOUTH. Only five common words have the UI spelling: FRUIT, JUICE, BRUISE, CRUISE, and SUIT. (You can mention FRUIT to your child; you'll cover JUICE in Stage 17 when you both look at how C can have an S sound.) The OE spelling (SHOE) and the OUGH spelling (THROUGH) are covered as exceptions or as "tricky" words in upcoming stages.

When you get a chance, look at Appendices P and Q together. They have similar information, but from opposite perspectives. Appendix P looks at the code from an encoding (spelling) perspective: hearing sounds, how might they be symbolized by letters? Appendix Q looks at the code from a decoding (reading) perspective: seeing letters, how might they be replaced by sounds? More succinctly: Appendix P is How to Spell a Sound; Appendix Q is How to Sound a Spelling. Much can be learned about the code and its complexities by studying these two appendices. They are only for you, not for your child. You'll continue presenting the code to your child as you have been doing: in a gradual, systematic, logical, and complete manner over these 18 stages.

Time to get your child started with the /ew/ sound: ZOO without the Z. Say (but do not yet write) the word MOON. Tell her the two of you are going to spell the word MOON together. Ask her what sound she can hear at the beginning of the word. When she answers /m/, the two of you can agree the first letter should be M. Write the M on an index card. Ask about the sound at the end of the word. When she tells you /n/, write the N, leaving space for the spelling of the vowel sound that must be in the middle:

M   N

Now ask her: what is the vowel sound in between the M sound and the N sound? (Remind her: all words have vowels.) Help her to isolate the /ew/ sound. Once she can make the sound correctly, discuss it with her: it's clearly a *new* vowel sound! Trouble is, we are out of vowels to spell the sound. In fact, our 5 vowels are already over-worked: they each make both a short and a long sound.

So how can the 2 of you spell this new sound? Tell her, fortunately, the problem has already been solved: this new vowel sound, /ew/, is spelled with a double O. Now add the OO in the space between the M and the N and let her see it: MOON. Discuss this with her: double O spells this new *single* sound, just as CH and SH spelled a single sound back in Stage 8. So, OO is another two-fer: two letters fer one sound – in this case, /ew/. CH and SH are consonant two-fers; OO is a vowel two-fer. Below where you have written MOON, write some similar words. Can she figure them out on her own?

> MOON
> SOON
> SPOON
> BALLOON
> TOOTH

This new sound undoubtedly fascinates her, so take her to Appendix L and turn her loose on the OO words under the /ew/ heading. Can she read most of the words she finds there? Help with any new vocabulary. Tell her that now she can see how the word YOU ought to be spelled: YOO. That's why YOU is tricky! Give special attention to TOO in this group, and compare it to the word TO (covered in Stage 9). These words sound the same, but they are spelled differently. Discuss the 2 meanings with her. Also, once she decodes the word COOL in the appendix, write SCOOL on an index card and have her read it. Tell her that SCHOOL is an irregular word (it has a silent H) and then add it to the appendix, spelling it correctly.

When the two of you have completed the OO group in the appendix, remind her that long A has two different spellings: A-E (MADE) and AI (RAIN). Long E does too: EE (SEEK) and EA (MEAT). Well, /ew/ has *four* different spellings! She has seen the first one: OO. Now she must learn the other three! Write the following 2 sentences and have her read them:

> His NOO bike just came from the bike shop.
> Her BLOO hat was on the chair in the kitchen.

Once she decodes these sentences, congratulate her and tell her /ew/ is spelled OO if that sound is in the *middle* of a word, for example, BROOM. But if the sound /ew/ comes at the *end* of a word, as it does in these 2 sentences, it is spelled EW or UE. (The words TOO and ZOO are obvious exceptions to this generalization.) Re-write the 2 above sentences correctly and add 2 more:

> His NEW bike just came from the bike shop.
> Her BLUE hat was on the chair in the kitchen.
> The witch FLEW on her BROOM stick.
> SUE ate her lunch with a SPOON.

So, OO, EW, and UE are all two-fers for the same sound, /ew/. After she ponders these sentences for a while, let her see the EW and UE word groups in Appendix L. Can she now decode most of these words? If she notices that LEWD and CRUEL ought to be spelled LOOD and CROOL (given the above rule), tell her she is absolutely correct!

Comment on the fact that the two boxed words, NEW and KNEW, are pronounced the same way. Discuss their different meanings and remind her that she has seen silent K before: KNOCK, KNOB, KNOT, KNIFE. Also, compare the earlier tricky word, DO, with DEW and DUE:

I DO my job. The DEW is on the grass. Mom is DUE home SOON.

The last spelling (for now) of /ew/ once again involves silent E. In these words, the /ew/ sound is again in the middle of the word, yet it is not spelled OO! Another quirk of English! Have your child decode these two sentences:

Where is my TOOB of tooth paste?
It is best to be NOOD when taking a bath!

Tell him TOOB and NOOD ought to be spelled this way (think of NOODLE) – but they're not. Rewrite them correctly and let him study the spellings:

Where is my TOOB of tooth paste?
It is best to be NOOD when taking a bath!
Where is my TUBE of tooth paste?
It is best to be NUDE when taking a bath!

When these words are spelled correctly, the work you both did in Stage 11 would indicate a long U sound. But the long U sound (YEW) is difficult to make when it follows /t/ or /n/. You can both try to pronounce these 2 words with a long U; it is difficult to do so! The sound /ew/ is *close* to long U, but not exact. (Compare TUBE and CUBE: sometimes /ew/ sounds better and sometimes /yew/ sounds better!)

Now let him see the whole list of U-E words in the appendix. For all of them, the U says /ew/. Help as needed. If you have a calendar nearby, show him the month of JUNE. The 9 boxed words with the heading "/y/ + /ew/" in the appendix *do* have the long U sound. Cover these 9 words, or omit them, as you see fit.

The next task is to teach your child the sound /oo/ as in the word BOOK. As the teacher, you need to hear how different OO sounds in a word like BOOK compared to MOON. OO is a correct spelling for 2 entirely different sounds, /ew/ and /oo/:

MOON = /m/ + /ew/ + /n/
BOOK = /b/ + /oo/ + /k/

Since this new sound /oo/ is also spelled with the two-fer OO, there will be plenty of room for your child to become confused here. Before moving on, make sure you can hear, and accurately produce, these two different vowel sounds.

***

Once you are ready, say, but do not yet write, the word BOOK. Your child has certainly heard this word before. Tell her the two of you are going to spell the word BOOK together. Ask her what sound she can hear at the beginning of the word. When she answers /b/, agree with her that the first letter should be B, and write it on a card. Ask about the sound at the end of the word. When she tells you /k/, write the K, leaving space for the spelling of the vowel sound in the middle:

B   K

Now ask her: what is the vowel sound between the B sound and the K sound? Help her to isolate the /oo/ sound. Once she can make the sound correctly, discuss it with her: it must be another new vowel sound!

So how shall the 2 of you spell this one? Here, you must give her the bad (or at least, confusing) news: this new sound is *also* spelled with a double O, just as she spelled /ew/ in MOON. Now add the OO in the space between the B and the K and let her see it: BOOK. Write some similar words below the word BOOK and see if she can decipher them on her own:

BOOK
LOOK
COOK
TOOK

Point out that the two-fer, OO, has two different sounds, just as each of the single vowels have two sounds! For example, just as E says both /e/ and /E/; OO says both /ew/ and /oo/. No big deal. Compare the two sounds of OO side by side with her:

MOON   BOOK
SOON   LOOK
NOON   COOK
SPOON   TOOK

For amusement, the 2 of you might give these 2 columns of words the other OO sound. What results is 8 unrecognizable "words"! Tell her she can always recall the two sounds of OO by remembering the phrase GOOD FOOD. (Given their spelling, these two words should rhyme. Clearly, they don't.) Now take her to the appendix and let her read the OO words starting with TOOK and BOOK.

Teacher Note: COULD, SHOULD, and WOULD rhyme with GOOD. They ought to be spelled COOD, SHOOD, and WOOD. Alas, these words are "tricky." You'll deal with them in Stage 15.

That leaves the 2 exceptions I have listed in the appendix: FLOOD and BLOOD. They have neither the /ew/ nor the /oo/ sound. They have, instead, an /u/ sound:

$$BLOOD = /b/ + /l/ + /u/ + /d/$$
$$FLOOD = /f/ + /l/ + /u/ + /d/$$

Make her aware of these two exceptions; both are common words.

I suggest the following test before moving on. On index cards, write 5-6 double O words with the /oo/ sound, 5-6 double O words with the /ew/ sound, and the words BLOOD and FLOOD. Shuffle the cards and see how she does. You'll test the other spellings of /ew/ (EW, UE, and U-E) a little further below.

Teacher Note: Here is an interesting aside for you as teacher (I wouldn't cover it with the beginning reader.) The words BULL, FULL, and PULL should also be in this /oo/ group, along with WOOL. All 4 words rhyme. Note the difference in vowel sound between these words and the following three: DULL, GULL, and HULL. The latter 3 are spelled correctly because their vowel sound is /u/. So why aren't BULL, FULL, and PULL spelled logically, like WOOL, with the double O? Answer: Those spellings are already taken by the words BOOLEAN (a type of logic), FOOL, and POOL. These words, of course, have the /ew/ sound.

Next, ask him to name the first sound in the word BOY (don't write anything yet). Then ask him to say BOY without that initial B sound. Help him, if necessary, to isolate the sound /oy/. That's the next new vowel sound! Tell him /oy/ is spelled OY at the *end* of a word. Now write these 4 words on a piece of paper. Can he read them? Define SOY and COY if necessary.

BOY   TOY   SOY   COY

Emphasize that each of these words has only two sounds: the initial consonant sound plus the OY sound. OY, like SH and OO, is a two-fer, not a blend. As part of a two-fer, the sound of Y is nothing like its sound in the words YELL and YES. OY, like all two-fers, must be recognized, at a glance, as a special letter combination that makes a single sound, in this case, /oy/.

Now, tell him /oy/ is spelled OI, not OY, if that sound occurs in the *middle* of a word (or syllable). Write these 4 words with the four you've already written:

BOY	TOY	SOY	COY
BOIL	TOIL	SOIL	COIL

Can he read them? Stress that OI is simply a second spelling (a different two-fer) for the sound /oy/. The two of you can agree that, while COYN (for instance) may be perfectly readable, COIN is the correct spelling. Now help him work through the OY and OI word groups in the appendix. If you must hide parts of a word to help him decode it, don't split the O from the I (or the O from the Y). For example, you could gradually uncover the word POINT this way: POI (CV), POIN (CVC), POINT (CVCC). Help with the two-syllable words as needed.

Reminder: Our earlier rule, "when two vowels go walking, the first does the talking," does *not* work with any of the new vowel combinations in this stage. Remind him when that rule *does* work: only for the 4 vowel combinations AI, EA, EE, and OA (see Stage 11).

I suggest you use the word NOW to introduce her to the next new sound. Get the first sound of the word from her: /n/. Now ask her to repeat the word without the N sound: /ow/. It's the sound we make when we suddenly feel some pain: OWWW! When she has correctly isolated the sound, tell her this is indeed another new vowel sound, and it's spelled OW when it happens at the *end* of a word. Write out a few simple examples:

NOW	COW	HOW

Emphasize there are only two sounds in these words: the initial consonant sound and the vowel sound, /ow/. The OW letter combination, another two-fer, makes a single sound, /ow/, just as OY, above, made the single sound /oy/.

In the *middle* of a word, /ow/ is usually spelled by the two-fer OU instead of OW. Write some examples for her to see, beneath the above words. Knowing that OU also says /ow/, can she decipher these 3 words?

NOW	COW	HOW
NOUN	COUCH	HOUND

If necessary, show HOUND gradually: HOU (CV), HOUN (CVC), HOUND (CVCC). When you show her the appendix, do the OW words first. They are a little easier than the OU words and they involve only 3 rhyming groups. If she has trouble with any word in these 2 groups, take the time to write the word on an index card and hide parts of it with your finger to help her along. Don't be in a hurry –

some of these words are quite difficult for a beginner.

I have 3 exceptions listed in this category: GROUP, SOUP, and YOUTH. Tell her they *ought* to be spelled with OO instead of OU – that may allow her to identify all three of them. OU is an uncommon spelling for /ew/.

> **Teacher Note**: At this point, you may want to take a moment to review, all the two-letter combinations (two-fers) she has seen so far. As you write each one of the following, ask her to make the correct sound: CH, SH, TH, OO (has 2 answers), EW, OY, UE, OU, OI, OW. Review as necessary.

Next, have him focus on the spoken word JAW. Get the first sound of the word from him, /j/, and ask him to repeat the word without the J sound: /aw/. It's the sound we make when we see a cute baby or puppy: AWWW! Once he has the correct sound isolated, tell him it's another new vowel sound. It's spelled AW at the *end* of a word. Write the following:

> JAW   PAW   LAW

and let him read them. Compare the /aw/ sound to /ew/, /oo/, /oy/, and /ow/; the two of you can agree it's a new vowel sound.

When the sound /aw/ occurs in the *middle* of a word, it's usually spelled AU instead of AW. Write the following:

> JAW   PAW   LAW
> JAUNT   PAUL   LAUNCH

Help with both pronunciation and meaning as necessary. (These words are harder than most!) When you show him the groupings in the appendix, do the AW words first – they are easier, more common, and more amenable to rhyme. The AU group docs not have many common words, but I believe they are worth doing, especially for an older student.

The words listed in the appendix as "other" all have one thing in common: the letter A followed by an L. You presented one of these groups to your child back in Stage 8 (the ALL group) because it had so many common words. Having a single A, all these words look like they should have the short A sound: /a/. However, in English, when the letter A is followed by an L, the A often says /aw/ rather than /a/. (Exceptions: Alabama, alfalfa, allergy, Algebra, alimony.)

Time to Evaluate: The two of you have just finished covering 5 new vowel sounds – and each of them had multiple spellings (11 total). Let's sum all this up in a (hopefully) amusing manner for your child. Write the following sentences and let her read them (with some help as needed):

4 /ew/ sounds:	Sue threw a prune in the lagoon.
5 /oo/ sounds:	Look! That crook took my book! What a shnook!
4 /oy/ sounds:	That boy enjoys his coins and toys.
5 /ow/ sounds:	Wow! How loud that brown cow MOOS!
5 /aw/ sounds:	Paul saw a small ball at the mall.

A more serious test: Take 3 common words from each of the 11 spellings, place them on index cards, shuffle them, and see how she does. If you notice any significant weaknesses, take the time to go back and review.

The R-controlled vowel sounds, /ar/, /or/, and /er/, are in thousands of common words. My experience is that children have less trouble with these sounds than they have with the above five. As teacher, note for yourself how the sound of the vowel reverts to its short sound in each of the following pairs of words, if you remove the R: CART – CAT, PERT – PET, BIRD – BID, SHORT – SHOT, and BURN – BUN.

Do /ar/ first with your child. Say, but don't yet write, the word CAR. To spell this word, ask him for the first sound he hears. He should reply /k/. So, the first letter in the spelling should be C or K. Write the C and stop:

C

Now ask him to say CAR but without the C sound. Help, if necessary, to isolate the sound /ar/. Discuss this new sound with him. This sound is the actual *name* of the letter R. Could this be the spelling?   (write the R next to the C)

CR

If he is okay with this spelling, remind him: all words must have a vowel. CR, alone, is simply the initial blend in words like CREEP, CRIB, and CRAB. CR can't be the way to spell CAR. Does he hear any short vowel sounds (/a/ /e/ /i/ /o/ /u/) in this word? No. Any long vowel sounds? No. So simply inform him: /ar/ is a new sound and it's spelled AR. Cross out CR and write it correctly:

~~CR~~
CAR

Emphasize the following points with him. AR is another two-fer: the two letters make the single sound, /ar/. AR is not a blend of either of A's sounds (/a/ or /A/) with /r/. (Note: The letter R and its sound, /r/, are tricky in English: R is the only consonant that *always* changes the sound of a single-letter vowel if it *follows* that vowel.) Write some words under the word CAR, and see if he can read them:

CR
CAR
CART
FAR
FART
BAR
BARN
BARK

Now go to Appendix L and let him read the words in the AR group. Transfer problem words to an index card and hide letters with your finger only if needed.

Teacher Note: The exceptions in the AR group, WAR and WARM, are actually pronounced WOR and WORM. Looking ahead, the 5 exceptions in the OR group are actually pronounced WERD, WERK, WERST, WERLD, and WERM. Thus, all the exceptions in this part of the appendix should be in the *following group*.

Next up: the new sound /or/. Tell her the two of you will write a sentence together: "I have a new toy for you." All these words, except the word FOR, are decodable, or they were on a previous tricky word list. Allowing her to do as much as she can on her own, get the following written:

I HAVE A NEW TOY   YOU.

Now ask her: how shall we spell the word FOR? She should be able to get the initial F. Once she does, write it:

I HAVE A NEW TOY   F   YOU.

Now ask her to say FOR, but without the F sound. When she has correctly isolated the /or/ sound, ask her how she thinks it should be spelled. Remind her that the sound /ar/, above, was spelled AR. If she gets it, fine; if not, tell her it is spelled with a new two-fer: OR. Complete the spelling:

I HAVE A NEW TOY FOR YOU.

As you did earlier with AR, discuss this new two-fer with her. It has a single sound – and that sound is not a blend /o/ and /r/. Write these words (and pseudo words) under FOR and see how she does:

I HAVE A NEW TOY FOR YOU.
FORT

COR
CORN
SOR
SORT
NOR
NORTH

Assuming she can read these, show her that, in the appendix, there are two spellings listed for the sound /or/: OR and ORE. In the ORE spelling, the final E is silent. Have her read through these two groups of words, helping as needed with pronunciation or meaning.

Teacher Note: The last sound in this admittedly lengthy stage is /er/. In this case, she already knows (from Stage 9) an important word with this sound: HER. It turns out HER is not a tricky word at all. In fact, it's perfectly phonetic. I included it on the first tricky word list solely because I wanted to have *all* the possessives (my, your, yours, his, her, hers, our, ours, their, theirs) for early sentence construction.

Given that your child already knows the word HER, I suggest you approach this final sound as follows. Ask her if she remembers how to spell HER from Stage 9. Once she has it, write it on some paper. Ask her to repeat the word, but without the H sound: ER. Write this as well:

HER
ER

So, just as the sound /ar/ is spelled AR, and /or/ is spelled OR, /er/ is spelled ER. Point out that the sound of the vowel in HER is neither short nor long. (It's impossible to pronounce HER with a short E – and if she pronounces it with a long E, she will say the word HERE.) ER is another two-fer: a unique sound in English. Let her know that this sound, and its spelling, ER, are found in lots of words. Under the words HER and ER, write the following pseudo words:

HER
ER
TER
MER
FER
PER
VER

After she reads these, and agrees they are not words, go back and add some letters to make each of them a word:

HER
PER
BUTTER
SUMMER
FERN
PEPPER
CLEVER

When you go to the appendix, show her there are 3 spellings for the sound /er/: ER, IR, and UR. Point out how PERK, IRK, and LURK rhyme! So do BERT, DIRT, and HURT! Ditto for PERCH, BIRCH, and CHURCH. What a weird language, right? Many of the words in these groups are boxed as high-frequency words, so give them some special attention. Phonetically, the word GIRL could just as well have been spelled GERL or GURL. Only practice and experience will allow your child to master the correct spelling of a word when there is more than one possible phonetic spelling.

Final evaluation: Make a small 12-card deck with the following two-fers written (one per card): CH, SH, TH, OO, EW, UE, OY/OI, OW/OU, AW/AU, AR, OR, ER/IR/UR. On the back of each of these 12 cards, write a word that uses the two-fer: CHIP, SHIP, THIN, GOOD/FOOD, CHEW, BLUE, BOY/BOIL, OW! /OUCH!, PAW/PAUL, CAR, FOR, BERT/DIRT/HURT. Show her the first side of the card and see if she can make the proper sound(s) of the two-fer. If needed, show her the second side with the word(s) that uses the two-fer's sound. Stay with this until she knows these two-fers thoroughly.

Teacher Note: Back in Stage 6, you'll recall we put off reading 16 *ending* blends involving the letter R: RB, RD, RF, RG, RK, RL, RM, RN, RP, RT, RST, RCH, RSH, RTH, RVE, and RSE. Do we have to do these now? Good news! They're already done! If you look at the AR, OR, ER, IR, and UR word lists in Appendix L, you'll see we just covered all these ending blends.

Stage 14
Words Ending in Long Vowel Sounds
Y as a Vowel

Y ou and your child have now studied 40 of the 41 sounds in the English language (only voiced /SH/ remains). However, he has not yet seen all the ways in which those sounds can be symbolized by letters. He saw in Stage 11 that he could spell /E/ as EE (MEET) or as EA (SEAT). He saw in Stage 13 he could spell /ew/ as OO (MOON), as UE (BLUE), or as EW (GREW). In this stage, he'll study new spellings for all the long vowel sounds. These new spellings occur when the long vowel sound is at the *end* of a word. He'll also see how the letter Y can act as a stand-alone vowel as well as a consonant.

The Spelling Corner – As you work through this stage with your child, choose words from Stage 13 for your informal spelling practice. As you recall, most of the sounds in that stage have two (or more) spellings; that will make her spelling task more challenging now. Remind her that the spelling of a vowel sound often differs, depending on whether that sound is at the end, or in the middle of a word. Don't expect perfection. The ER/IR/UR group is especially problematic. If she spells CHURCH as CHERCH (rhymes with PERCH) or as CHIRCH (rhymes with BIRCH), praise her for her phonetic ingenuity, but then correct HER/HIR/HUR.

Start by reviewing with your child the two spellings he knows for long A: A-E (as in WAKE) and AI (as in SAIL). Explain that these spellings are used when the long A sound occurs in the *middle* of a word. If the long A sound occurs at the *end* of a word, something that has not yet happened, he must spell it with a new two-fer: AY. Write these 4 words for him as examples:

BAY	SAY	JAY	PLAY

Can he read them? The first 3 words have only 2 sounds each. Once he is comfortable with these words, review the OY sound by writing these four words below them:

BAY	SAY	JAY	PLAY
BOY	SOY	JOY	PLOY

Easy, right? OY says /oy/ while AY says /A/. Now go to Appendix M where I have the most common AY words listed. The spelling of WEDNESDAY is slightly irregular given its pronunciation: /w/ + /e/ + /n/ + /z/ + /d/ + /A/. Otherwise,

I don't see any problematic words on this list. See if your child can read this group directly from the appendix. When finished, he has 3 spellings for the sound /A/: A-E, AI, AY.

Review with your child the 2 spellings she has for /O/: O-E (HOME) and OA (BOAT). Explain that these spellings are used when the long O sound occurs in the *middle* of a word. If /O/ occurs at the *end* of a word, there are three additional ways to spell it! You and your child can find these 3 spellings (O, OW, and OE) in Appendix M. Focus first on the O words. Have her compare the first 3 words there (GO, NO, SO) with the 3 exceptions at the bottom of that column (TO, DO, WHO). GO, NO, and SO are spelled correctly; TO, DO, and WHO are irregular. That's why they were tricky words back in Stage 9. All 6 should rhyme, but they don't! Have her go through the remainder of this O list, helping as needed. When finished, she has 3 spellings for /O/: O-E, OA, and O.

The OW spelling of /O/ will cause some confusion for a while. He just saw, in Stage 13, that the two-fer, OW, was a spelling for /ow/. Now he needs to learn OW is also a common spelling for /O/. I recommend that you list both sounds of the two-fer OW side by side for your child so that he can see (and hear) for himself, that this two-fer, just as OO in the previous stage, has two different sounds:

OW spells /ow/	OW spells /O/
cow	low
how	slow
vow	blow
now	know
chow	snow
wow	mow
plow	glow
brow	crow
pow!	flow
bow	bow
town	grown

This is enough to confuse anyone! The only thing to do is to point it out, explicitly, to your child. The 2 of you can have some fun with these 22 words by pronouncing them the other way. It most cases, the result is not a known word.

Note, however, if the first sound is /n/, the resulting word can be pronounced either way: NOW, KNOW. And, of course, BOW can be pronounced both ways: BOW of a ship, BOW and arrow. I would write these 22 words on index cards along with the six words NO, GO, SO, TO, DO, and WHO. Mix the 28 cards and stay with it until your child gets them correct. Having passed this test, he should have no major problems reading the other words in the OW list in the appendix. Pay special attention to KNOW, KNOWS, OWN, and KNOWN – four important, high-frequency words.

The last spelling of long O (for now) is the least important one: OE. The 2 of you can see in the appendix that there are only about a half-dozen words in this group. The most important one is GOES. Your child already knows it as a tricky word from Stage 12. TOE, TOES, and the exception, SHOES, are also words he should know.

Before going any further with your child, let's discuss the most versatile letter of all: Y. Uniquely, this letter can act either as a consonant or as a stand-alone vowel. At the *beginning* of a word, Y acts as a consonant. It has the sound your child already knows in words like YARD, YELLOW, and YES. At the *end* of a word, however, Y always acts as a vowel. As a stand-alone vowel, Y has 2 possible sounds: /E/ (CANDY) and /I/ (CRY).

W, too, sometimes acts as a vowel – in the word LAW, for instance. But, in that word, AW is a digraph (a two-fer); the W is inseparable from the vowel A. Likewise, in the words BOY and DAY, OY and AY are digraphs; the Y is inseparable from the vowel preceding it. The letter Y, however, *by itself*, often acts as a vowel. In the word, CANDY, Y is the only vowel in the second syllable; in CRY, Y is the *only* vowel.

Here are two useful facts you'll be teaching your child shortly. First, for any one-syllable word in which Y is the *only* vowel, Y says /I/. Examples: MY, CRY, TRY. Note: BOY and DAY do not violate this rule because Y is not the only vowel in those words. Second, for nearly all multi-syllable words *ending* in a stand-alone vowel Y (thousands of words), Y says /E/. Check out the appropriate sections in Appendix M for yourself.

Getting back to instruction, review the consonant Y with your child by having him read a few words that start with Y: YES, YARD, YAWN, YUCK, and YELLOW. Also, remind him that every syllable in every word must have a vowel. Now give him the surprising news: Y can sometimes act as a vowel. It's the only letter in the alphabet that can act as either a consonant or a stand-alone vowel. In fact, tell him he's already seen this happen with one of the tricky words he already knows. Can he remember which one? (MY in Stage 9). In the word MY, the letter Y clearly has the long I sound.

So, it turns out that MY is not a tricky word at all! There are lots of one-syllable words in English just like MY. Take him to the appendix and show him a whole list of such words. Armed with this knowledge that Y can act as a vowel that spells /I/, he should be able to read these 16 words with little trouble. Acknowledge that the U in BUY and GUY is a little weird. Also, explain the difference between BY and BUY. Add the new interrogative (WHY) to your child's growing list of important "question words."

Once he is comfortable with the above, have him check out the other spelling of long I in the appendix. IE is a rare spelling of /I/, but those are 4 common words he should know. Summing up, your child now has three ways to spell /I/: I-E (HIDE), Y (MY), and IE (PIE).

Review with your child the 3 spellings she has (so far) for /E/: EE (SPEED), EA (HEAT), and E-E (STEVE). These spellings are used when the long E sound occurs in the *middle* of a word. However, if the long E sound occurs at the *end* of a word, there are three additional ways to spell it, two of which are new. You already looked at one of these spellings back in Stage 8 where you studied the E/EE group of rhyming words. I have reproduced that group here, in Appendix M. Simply do a quick review of these short words. This time I included some two-syllable words as well.

Now tell her there are two *new* ways to spell the long E sound when it occurs at the end of a word – and they both involve the letter Y acting as a vowel. Write these 2-syllable words and ask her to read them:

> PUPPEE
> CANDEE
> MOMMEE

She can probably read these, given that she just reviewed the E/EE group of words. Tell her that, for BIG words (2 or more syllables), English uses Y instead of EE at the end of a word. Now write the correct spelling next to the 3 words she just read:

> PUPPEE   PUPPY
> CANDEE   CANDY
> MOMMEE   MOMMY

With this Y = EE equality fresh in her head, go to the appendix and spend as much time as necessary having her decode the large group of words that start with thc word BELLY. I purposely made this a large group. It acts as a good review of many of the sounds the 2 of you have already covered – and most of the two-fers are represented here. I picked words that should be known even to the youngest child.

Teacher Note. The rule for this section is as follows: for two (or more) syllable words, an ending Y says /E/. There are 7 exceptions listed at the end of the Y group in the appendix. Note that, apart from JULY, these exceptions are all verbs. They are not the only exceptions. I think a child should learn the 7 I've listed. An adult learner, however, should also be exposed to the following larger group of exceptions. They are all verbs and they all end in IFY: TERRIFY, HORRIFY, UNIFY, MODIFY, NOTIFY, VERIFY, VILIFY, CLARIFY, DIGNIFY, FORTIFY, TESTIFY, SATISFY, JUSTIFY, QUALIFY, and SIGNIFY. For all these verb exceptions, ending Y says /I/.

In longer words, a final /E/ sound is sometimes spelled with the digraph EY rather than with Y alone. Show him this group in the appendix (starting with the word KEY). This is not a common situation. In reading these words, he can simply pretend the E is not there – then these words could have been in the large group of Y words he just finished. You can decide if you want to cover the 5 words listed as "exceptions" in this group. One of them, THEY, was already covered as a tricky word back in Stage 9. The other 4 exceptions are not common words.

Before moving on, do the following short exercise with your child as a review. The three groupings, below, show how Y acts *with* a vowel, or *as* a vowel, in one-syllable words. Paired with O or A, Y is part of a two-fer: an unbreakable unit that makes a single sound. Simply let him read through these groups and make sure there are no problems.

AY says /A/	OY says /oy/	Y says /I/
day	boy	my
pay	toy	by
play	soy	cry
stay	coy	why
say	joy	try
way	ploy	fry
may	Roy	dry

Easy, right? In multi-syllable words, ending Y says /E/. In single-syllable words, an ending Y falls into one of the above 3 categories.

Adding the suffix, ING, to words that end in Y is simple: tack it on! Go to the appendix and show her the box labeled "Adding ING" and let her read these words.

Adding the suffix, Y, to a word often changes it from a noun (SOAP) to an adjective (SOAPY). Adding the suffix, LY, often changes an adjective (LOUD) to an adverb (LOUDLY). The rules governing these processes make it a bit trickier than adding ING. Look in Appendix M for the groups labeled "Adding Y" and "Adding LY." If you examine those sections together, the 2 of you will notice:

- Often, a Y can simply be added to a word without any changes.
- If the original word ends in a silent E, drop the E before adding Y.
- If the original word has a single, short vowel followed by a single consonant, double the consonant and add the Y.
- Like ING, LY can usually be tacked on without any other changes.

You and your child can also take a brief look in the appendix at how to form the plural of words ending in Y, AY, or OY. It's simple: if the *only* vowel in a word (or syllable) is Y, we make that word plural by changing the Y to an I and adding ES. In all cases, the final S has a /z/ sound.

You have one final topic to do here in Stage 14. In multi-syllable words, one syllable is usually stressed more (spoken louder) than the other(s). Give your child some examples of this phenomenon. Let him see these two lists where the stressed syllable is in uppercase:

First syllable stressed	Second syllable stressed
CARton	carTOON
BUTton	balLOON
FLOWer	aWAKE
KITten	beTWEEN
GIVen	supPORT
MOMmy	deMAND
FOGgy	aVOID

If he has trouble hearing the syllable that is stressed, pronounce the word the other way: kitTEN, for instance. It sounds funny, right?

Speak some longer words and see if he can tell you which syllable gets the most stress: aMERica, PUNishment, ENemy, umBRELla, kangaROO. volunTEER, baNAna, SUpercaliFRAgilisticexpialiDOcious. You can easily include more words if he needs extra practice.

Next, show him how syllable stress affects the sounds of the vowels in the *unstressed* syllables. Call this phenomenon Lazy Vowel. Of the 17 vowel sounds in the English language, the two that require the least effort to pronounce are /i/ and /u/. To make those 2 sounds, you barely need to open your mouth.

It turns out that, in countless English words, the sound of the vowel in the *unstressed* syllable, *no matter what that vowel happens to be*, defaults to either /u/ or /i/. Here are 3 examples: ALARM, APART, VANILLA. Notice that the leading A in ALARM and APART – and both A's in VANILLA – are in unstressed syllables. The sound of these A's defaults to a short U sound: uh/LARM, uh/PART, Vuh/NIL/luh. If you try to pronounce these 3 words with the short A sound you hear in APPLE, you'll get some awkward results.

If you look in the appendix, you'll find other examples of this phenomenon; it's a common occurrence in unstressed syllables. Note that both A's in AMERICA are lazy because the accent in this word is on the second syllable. I include PIZZA in the appendix as well. The spelling is hopelessly non-phonetic (should be PEETSA) but every child needs to know this word!

This Lazy Vowel phenomenon commonly occurs in words ending in AL or EL. In both cases, the sound degenerates into a simple "ULL." You and your child can see what I mean by examining the words at the end of Appendix M. It's simply a common way of dealing with vowels in unstressed syllables.

While many cases of Lazy Vowel involve vowels defaulting to a lazy U, I have included other words (there are thousands!) in the appendix where the unstressed vowel defaults to a lazy I instead of a lazy U. Compare the ENT sound in the words CONSENT and ABSENT. In the second word, ENT is in the unstressed syllable and the pronunciation is closer to ABSINT. Here are two other examples:

ATLAS = /a/ + /t/ + /l/ + /i/ + /s/.
LEMON = /l/ + /e/ + /m/ + /i/ + /n/

This whole Lazy Vowel phenomenon is easy to understand: why make the effort to properly pronounce a vowel in an unstressed syllable? Just sort of mumble a short U or a short I and be done with it. It makes our speech more efficient. I wouldn't make too big a deal over this topic. If your child insists on pronouncing these words phonetically, without defaulting to short U or short I in an unstressed syllable, that's fine. It won't affect her reading in any significant way. It's just something a beginning reader should know UhBOUT.

Stage 15
Reading Sentences (Part III)

This is the final time your child will be restricted to reading carefully constructed decodable text. The next time he sees full sentences (Stage 18) he'll be an independent reader – able to read unrestricted text from any age-appropriate book. You're getting close to the finish line.

In this stage, your child will complete his study of the 50 most-used, yet irregular words of the English language. You started this process when you introduced 12 tricky words to him in Stage 9. You added 19 new words in Stage 12. Below, you'll find the final 19 tricky words that will get his total to fifty. In this current list, both the previous lists are included.

Tricky Words (50)					
you	do	her	they	my	to
who	our	their	your	have	from
are	was	were	say	says	said
go	goes	come	give	what	where
one	of	been	does	gone	because
		done			
two	would	there	some	whose	four
could	move	put	want	eight	should
woman	once	love	watch	above	only
		sure			

Looking over this list, you can now see it has five words that have recently become perfectly phonetic. HER and OUR became phonetic in Stage 13; MY, GO, and SAY did the same in Stage 14. FROM, BEEN, BECAUSE, and SAID are almost perfectly phonetic. Eleven of the words on this list are simple to recognize if you ignore the final E: HAV, GIV, AR, GON, WER, DON, SOM, COM, GON, ABOV, and LOV.

Most of these words are among anyone's list of the 100 most-used words in the English language. I have included one such list in Appendix U, from the Oxford English dictionary. If you examine that list, you'll see 75% of the words are perfectly phonetic. The ones that are not, are included in my Tricky 50 list. The claim is often made (www.highfrequencywords.org) that knowing the 100 most-used words in English will give the reader access to approximately 50% of the text he'll ever be required to read. Whether the claim is true or not, the 50 words I have singled out as "tricky" are indeed important for your child's reading fluency.

Here are the criteria I used in constructing the sentences following later in this stage:

- All the previous criteria from Stage 9 and Stage 12 plus...
- Any word on the above Tricky 50 list
- Any word having one of the new 8 vowel sounds covered in Stage 13
- Any word ending in a long vowel sound, including all the new spellings from Stage 14
- Any interrogative
- Any preposition
- Any word that is phonetic based on what we have already covered.
- The spelled form of any number from 1 to 999,999.

Once again, write the 19 new words on index cards and spread them out on the table for her. On a piece of paper, write out the names of the numbers she can already read. Your paper should look like this:

1 – one	2 –	3 – three
4 –	5 – five	6 – six
7 – seven	8 –	9 – nine
10 – ten		

Tell her that the names of the missing numbers are among the cards in front of her and that she should figure it out for herself. If she needs help, show her how to use the available phonetic hints: the number 2 starts with the /t/ sound, 4 starts with an /f/ sound, and 8 ends with a /t/ sound. Once she has picked out the correct cards, make the following points:

- TWO is the only TW word in English with a silent W (compare TWIN, TWIST, TWIG, TWEET, TWEEZERS). It's crazy that this word has a W – but that's the hand we've been dealt! Discuss the difference in meaning between TO, TWO, and TOO with her.
- Given its spelling, FOUR ought to rhyme with OUR, but it doesn't. Given its pronunciation, it ought to be spelled FORE. That's why it's tricky!
- EIGHT is one of the goofiest spellings in English. The only phonetic thing about it is the final T. It ought to be spelled ATE, but unfortunately, that

spelling is already taken. Discuss the difference in meaning between ATE and EIGHT.

Remove the 3 number names from the pile of cards, and tell her there are 3 words that rhyme in the remaining cards. Let her pick out WOULD, COULD, and SHOULD based on their spellings. (Note: if she picks out MOVE, LOVE, and ABOVE, tell her you'll do those a little later!) With COULD, SHOULD, and WOULD in front of her, tell her they all rhyme with the word GOOD. Can she now say what they are? Can she use them in a sentence? Write the following sentences for her to read; they may help her understand the subtle differences in the meanings of these 3 words:

- WOULD you sing with me?   (are you willing to?)
- COULD you sing with me?   (are you able to?)
- SHOULD you sing with me?   (is it wise to?)

Ask how these 3 words SHOULD be spelled (WOOD, COOD, SHOOD). Their OU spelling (with a silent L!) is what makes them tricky. Three more cards off the table – 13 to go.

Ask her what the opposite (or complement!) of MAN is. If she doesn't know the word, tell her what it is and let her search for it. She should notice that the word MAN is part of the word WOMAN. Help with the correct pronunciation if necessary. It ought to be spelled WOOMIN – with the OO two-fer corresponding to /oo/, not /ew/. The two of you can try pronouncing this word with a short O or a long O – that will quickly demonstrate why it is "tricky." (The fact that the second, unstressed syllable in WOMAN is pronounced MIN is another example of Lazy Vowel.) Let her read the following:

- That WOMAN across the street is my mom's sister.
- Where is the WOMAN who lost her purse? Tell her I found it!

Now tell her there are 3 other words that *ought* to rhyme, and help her pick them out: MOVE, LOVE, and ABOVE. Does she recognize LOVE if you hide the E? Write these sentences for her to read:

- Mom, I LOVE you so much!
- He LOVES to go to the zoo!
- We LOVE milk and cake!
- The ground is below. The sky is ABOVE.
- My nose is ABOVE my mouth.

OK, so LOVE and ABOVE do rhyme. Can she tell you how they ought to be spelled? (LUV and ABUV). Ask her if she thinks the third card (MOVE) also rhymes? Get her to see that it can't rhyme because /m/ + /u/ + /v/ is not a word. In addition, MOVE probably doesn't rhyme with COVE and STOVE because it's a tricky word! Can she figure out what it is? Let her read these:

- MOVE your bike!   It's blocking the steps!
- When did you MOVE here with your family?

Agree with her that the phonetic spelling of MOVE should be MOOV. Nine cards remain on the table.

Tell her there is another question word in the group to go with the ones she already knows (WHEN, WHICH, WHO, WHAT, WHERE, HOW, WHY). Can she pick it out? Compare WHO and WHOSE side-by-side with her. They sound identical except that the additional S in WHOSE has (as is often the case) a Z sound. Here are some sentences to have her read:

- WHOSE book is this?   Its Mike's book.
- WHOSE hat is on the desk?   That hat belongs to Beth.

It ought to be spelled HOOZ, right? Retire the card and write all eight question words on a single sheet of paper for quick reference. Hang it on a wall so she sees it frequently.

Pick out the word PUT and remark that if it rhymed with NUT it wouldn't be a tricky word! Write some sentences to help her figure out the word from context:

- For the last time, PUT your toys away!
- Do not PUT your finger in your nose! It's rude!
- PUT the dog outside. He needs to pee.

PUT rhymes with FOOT and SOOT, so it ought to be spelled POOT.

COME is a tricky word from Stage 12. One of the remaining words rhyme with it. Let her pick it out.

- May I have SOME more milk?
- SOME dogs bark too much!
- SOMETHING is wrong with my bike.

SOME should be spelled SUM. Take time to discuss with her the difference between the words SOME and SUM. Six cards to go.

Pick up the card WANT. It's a tricky word, so it will not rhyme with GRANT and CAN'T. Maybe he can figure it out from context:

- Mom, I WANT to go to the store with you!
- Do you WANT more jelly on your toast?
- WHY are you yelling? WHAT do you WANT?

So, it's tricky because it ought to be spelled WUNT (rhymes with STUNT).

Write the word THEIR on a card and ask him to read it. It's from the first Tricky Word list in Stage 9. Tell him that in the five cards remaining, there is a word pronounced exactly the same as THEIR! (Not a rhyming word, but an exact equivalent.) When he picks it out, agree this is an unusual thing in English: two words spelled differently, sounding the same, but with different meanings. (Like SUN and SON, or TWO and TOO.) Use these sentences:

- Your book is over THERE on the shelf.
- THERE goes my sister! Do you think she saw us?
- THEIR cat ran away yesterday!
- THEIR home is at the top of the hill.

Both words are pronounced as THARE (or THAIR). THEIR indicates *possession*: their dog, their yard, their food. THERE indicates the *position* of something (or someone). It's the opposite of HERE: Here is your cup; I have it in my hand. vs. Your cup is up THERE on the top shelf.

He already knows the tricky word ONE from Stage 12. Tell him, from the 4 cards remaining, he should pick out the card likely to be pronounced in a similar manner: ONCE = ONE + /s/. Now have him read the following:

- ONCE upon a time, a witch rode her broom stick in the land of OZ.
- When frying an egg, you SHOULD flip it ONCE in the pan.
- You may go out to play ONCE you have eaten.

He may suspect WATCH will not rhyme with MATCH or CATCH because it's a tricky word. If he does not recognize the word, have him read the following sentences, pronouncing WATCH in a way that *does* rhyme with MATCH. I think he'll recognize the word:

- WATCH out Mac! You nearly ran into me!
- Would you like to WATCH a show with me?

To be regular, WATCH should be spelled WAWCH or WAUCH.

Tell him the word SURE is tricky only because it's missing a letter. If it were spelled SHURE (rhymes with LURE, CURE, and PURE) it wouldn't be tricky at all. So here he has the unusual case of S saying /sh/ instead of /s/. Have him read these sentences:

- Do you WANT to come with me? SURE I do!
- Are you SURE you saw him at the park?
- I SURE hope the rain stops soon!

To be phonetic, SURE should be spelled SHURE (or SHOOR). Point out that there is another common word where S says /sh/. Write SUGAR and see if he can read it. SUGAR should be spelled SHOOGER (rhymes with BOOGER).

Point to that last card on the table and say "Uh oh! ONLY one card left!" (If necessary, stress the word ONLY as you repeat the sentence.) Now have him read some sentences using this last word:

- I am ONLY FOUR, but I have a big sister who is ten.
- Am I the ONLY one in this room who can speak French?
- We need ONLY FOUR things in life: food, shelter, love, and beer!

Introducing these 19 new tricky words was a challenge, but the payoff will be substantial. Your child has now been exposed to the 45 most common, but phonetically irregular, words in the English language. I say 45 instead of 50 because, as I mentioned earlier, 5 of the words are now perfectly phonetic: HER, OUR, MY, GO, and SAY. Knowing these 45 words will be beneficial going forward because it will enable him to devote more energy to comprehension and less to decoding.

While the following exercise will take some time, it will improve your child's reading fluency. *Before* allowing him to read the decodable sentences below, prepare a special deck of flash cards containing all 45 Tricky Words. On one side of the card, print the word as it is actually spelled; on the other side, print the word as it *ought* to be spelled. See the box below. Consider letting your child help with this task; ask *him* how the word would be spelled if we all lived in Phonicsville.

Motivate your child by telling him this deck of cards has the trickiest words in our language. When he knows these words perfectly, he'll be an "expert" reader. When you practice with him, show only the side with the correct spelling (EIGHT). Show the phonetic side of the card (ATE) only if he needs it. <u>Caution</u>: In the phonetic spellings, OO can say either /ew/ or /oo/, just as it does in GOOD FOOD. When he can go through the entire group in under 3 minutes, he is ready to tackle the decodable sentences which follow.

Correct Spelling	Phonetic Spelling	Correct Spelling	Phonetic Spelling
above	abuv	said	sed
are	ar	says	sez
because	becuz	should	shood
been	bin	some	sum
come	cum	sure	shoor
could	cood	their	thair
do	doo	there	thair
does	duz	they	thay
done	dun	to	too
eight	ate	two	too
four	for	want	wunt
from	frum	was	wuzz
give	giv	watch	wawch
goes	goze	were	wer
gone	gawn	what	wut
have	hav	where	wair
love	luv	who	hoo
move	moov	whose	hooz
of	uv	woman	woomin
once	wuns	would	wood
one	wun	you	yoo
only	oanly	your	yoor
put	poot		

Decodable Sentences

I am proud that I can read!

The cow in the barn is mooing loudly. Maybe someone should milk her!

There is a toilet in our bathroom and a stove in our kitchen. These two rooms have a sink too!

Dad took my sister to the doctor because she has the flu.

Would you get a broom and help me clean this porch?

If you are thirsty, drink some lemonade.

Pass the salt and pepper please.

There is a bird chirping and singing in our birch tree. I think its a blue jay.

I just saw a shark in the surf!
Holy mackerel!
Not a mackerel, dude, a shark!

Do you want to throw a football around with me?

Here the river is wide and shallow, but up ahead, it grows narrow and deep.

That girl with a balloon is my sister. Her name is Emma.

My birthday is September 8. I am four years old. I was born on a Thursday.

Ben said, "Mom, do you love me?"
Mom said, "Oh Ben! I love you very much!"
"How much?" said Ben.
Then mom spread her arms far apart and said, "This much!"

My dog is in the back yard. He likes to play in the grass.

Mom says I must eat good food if I want to grow big and tall.

This rain is awful; I am sopping wet! Do you have a towel for me to dry off? Thank you!

I will get some flowers from our garden and put them in a vase.

Whose bike is on the porch? It should have a lock on it to keep it safe.

Where did this dirt on my shirt come from? I think a bird was at fault! Yuck!

When you eat, do you prefer a fork, a spoon, or a knife?

That boy standing there by the window took my book!

Yesterday was Sunday. I went to church with momma.

Dad did not like that new brand of beer. He threw the brew down the sink.

My brother put his computer on the shelf above his desk.

Its not polite to burp or fart in public!

Would you help me with my work? Its too difficult for me to do alone!

Could we have some popcorn for a snack?

I saw them at the playground. They were having a great time playing on the swing!

Do you have any more candy? Will you give me some?

Do you think we should go with Paul to the park?
No, we should stay home. Its too late to go out.

"What food do you like the best?" said Robert.
"I like pasta and meat balls best of all!" said Martha.

The woman sitting over there on the couch is my mother.

We are having corn on the cob, pork chops, and salad for dinner.

I cant swim with you now. I must watch my sister until my dad gets home.

The picnic will not happen this afternoon. I am sure its going to rain!

Is it true that Luke lost his new blue shoes?
Yes, but Sue found them.

A storm blew in from the west. There was some thunder and some hail.

There are only four girls in the van. Where are the other two girls?

Paula says that August is a hot month. Is that true?

Do you have any coins?
I have only eight dimes and four pennies.

Would you like to join our group? We read books together every Friday afternoon.

Do not spoil the party by being a grump!

"Why are you crying?" asked mom.
Sue said, "I am crying because I fell off my bike and hurt my elbow."

Do you enjoy playing with that boy? His name is Roy.
Heck no – he annoys me! He is too loud and he acts like a clown.

When lost in the woods, its a good plan to go north, south, east, or west.

I saw a hawk flying over our house.

"Billy, do not try to sit here and eat with such dirty hands!" said mom. "Go clean them – and use some soap!"

Who broke this window?
Sandy did. Its her fault. She threw the ball too hard. I could not catch it.

Hey Joe! Let me see your broken toe. How did it happen?
I was walking in bare feet and I hit my toe with a door. Ouch!

"Do you understand what will happen to you if you pick your nose in public?" said Aunt Bertha.
"Yes, I do," said LeRoy, "I will have a clean nose!"

Tell me a joke.
OK. When does a car have too much gas?
Answer: (Caution: silent W in 'answer')
When three kids are in the back seat.
Tell me another.
Why did the banana go to the doctor?
Answer: It did not peel well.

Do you know that if a duck flies upside down, its likely to quack up?

"Hey mom. Will the pie be very long?"
"No dear," said mom, "the pie will be very round."

Why are two and four afraid of seven?
Answer: Because seven eight nine.

Can you see the moon at noon?
Sometimes, but you can see the moon better when its dark.

Such a gloomy day this is! It makes me feel grouchy and grumpy, snarly and frumpy!

Teacher Note: A few nursery rhyme snippets...

Humpty Dumpty sat on a wall,
Humpty Dumpty had a great fall.
All the kings horses and all the queens men
could not put Humpty together again!

Are you sleeping? Are you sleeping? (feel free to sing!)
Brother Jon, Brother Jon?
Morning bells are ringing! Morning bells are ringing!
Ding, dang, dong. Ding, dang, dong.

Handsome Boy Blue, come blow your horn!
The sheeps in the meadow, the cows in the corn!
Where is the boy who looks after the sheep?
He's under a haystack, fast asleep!
Will you wake him?
No, not I! For if I do, he is sure to cry!

Oh, where have you been,
Billy Boy, Billy Boy?
Oh, where have you been,
Charming Billy?
I have been to seek a wife,
She's the joy of my life,
She's a pretty girl
Who will not leave her mother.

Baa, baa, black sheep,
Have you any wool?
Yes, sir, yes, sir,
Three bags full:
One for the master,

And one for the dame,
And one for the lovely girl
Who lives down the lane.

Teacher Note: What follows is optional. Do it only if you are both interested.

Do you know what numbers come after 10?
Yes, I do:

11 – eleven	16 – sixteen
12 – twelve	17 – seventeen
13 – thirteen	18 – eighteen
14 – fourteen	19 – nineteen
15 – fifteen	20 – twenty

But what comes after 20?
Its easy:

21 – twenty-one	26 – twenty-six
22 – twenty-two	27 – twenty-seven
23 – twenty-three	28 – twenty-eight
24 – twenty-four	29 – twenty-nine
25 – twenty-five	30 – thirty

Say, I think I see the pattern here! Is the next number 31 (thirty-one)?

Yes indeed! Here are the important numbers you will need to go all the way to 100 (one hundred):

40 – forty
50 – fifty
60 – sixty
70 – seventy

80 – eighty
90 – ninety
100 – one hundred

But what comes after one hundred (100)?

It all starts again: one hundred one (101), one hundred two (102), one hundred three (103) and so on – all the way to two hundred (200).

Then all the way to three hundred (300) and four hundred (400)?

Yes.

But what comes after nine hundred ninety-nine (999)?

One thousand (1000), one thousand one (1001), one thousand two (1002), and so on.

Do the numbers ever stop?

Nope. They go on forever! To infinity!

Stage 16
Unusual Spellings
Open and Closed Syllables

Here you'll be focusing your child's attention on some unusual spellings of the sounds /aw/, /I/, /f/, and /ch/. In addition, you'll help her with some common word families that, when mastered, will make independent reading much easier. Specifically, this stage includes:

- The -LE family (BOTTLE, SNUGGLE, WAFFLE).
- The irregular, but common, IGH, OUGH, and AUGH families (MIGHT, BOUGHT, CAUGHT).
- The PH spelling of /f/ (PHONE, GRAPH).
- The -TION family (ACTION, MENTION).
- The T spelling of /ch/ (FIXTURE, POSTURE)
- About two dozen words where the vowel, unexpectedly, has a LONG sound (COLD, FIND, WILD).
- An approach for analyzing multi-syllable words that helps to minimize pronunciation errors.

The Spelling Corner – The spelling you do with your child should now come from Stage 14 and Appendix M. These are tricky words for a beginner because most of the long vowel sounds have two or more plausible spellings. When you ask him to spell SLOW, for instance, does he say S-L-O, S-L-O-E, or S-L-O-W? (All these answers are phonetically correct, but only one is ultimately correct.) Remind him that a long A sound at the end of a word is always spelled AY. For a long E sound at the end of a word, the number of syllables helps decide if the word should end in E (FREE) or Y (BELLY). A long I sound at word's end is spelled Y (MY, CRY) but there are 4 exceptions: PIE, DIE, LIE, and TIE.

Throughout this stage, you'll be working with word lists in Appendix N. If you look there now (not with your child), you'll see that in the first group (the Giggle Group) all the words end in LE. What I have listed there is only a tiny sampling of the more than 3000 such words in the English language. Note that, for all the words in this group, the correct spelling *could* have been EL or AL instead of LE: APPEL, NOODEL, SIMPAL, PICKEL. In fact, that's exactly how a whole group of similar-sounding words *were* just spelled in Appendix M, for example, CAMEL, TUNNEL, MENTAL, and NICKEL. In other words, the entire GIGGLE Group is simply that many more examples of Lazy Vowel – a topic just discussed in Stage 14. The final sound for every one of these new words is ULL, the sound you can hear in the words DULL, HULL, and GULL.

To present the above to your child, first get him to pronounce /u/ + /l/ correctly. Do this by having him read the rhyming words GULL, HULL, and DULL (a bird, a ship's bottom, the opposite of sharp). With him sure of the sound of ULL, tell him lots of two and three-syllable words end with this exact same sound – but the spelling is LE instead of ULL. Show him this list of words on separate paper. On the left is the correct spelling; on the right is the way to say the word:

giggle = gig + GUL
sniffle = snif + FUL
puddle = pud + DUL
apple = ap + PUL
pebble = peb + BUL
puzzle = puz + ZUL
chuckle = chuc + KUL
turtle = tur + TUL
jungle = jung + UL

In pronouncing each of these words, he need only read the *first* syllable, and then add something that rhymes with "ULL." The E is silent. At the end of a word, LE is equivalent to UL: PICKLE = PIC/KUL. As he says each word, his tongue ends up touching the back of his upper teeth. He'll probably find this fun!

Once he seems to be catching on, take him to the appendix and turn him loose on the GIGGLE Group. If he has trouble with the three-syllable words listed there, like POSSIBLE, help him out by splitting it up for him: POS/SI/BLE. When finished with this group, tell him his phonics skills have now added another 3000 or so words to his I-can-read list!

The next topic, the GH groups in the appendix, will present more of a challenge for both of you. The spellings there are FRIGHTFUL. If brewers can market their beer, phonetically, as LITE, why must the rest of us spell it non-phonetically as LIGHT? I would tell you to skip the whole group, but it has far too many important and common words. I've divided them into 5 sub-groups in Appendix N. Four sounds, already introduced, will now get alternate spellings:

- IGH spells /I/
- AUGH and OUGH both spell /aw/
- EIGH spells /A/
- GH spells /f/

Start this new topic by asking your child to use her knowledge from Stage 11 to spell the word BITE. When she gets it, write it on some paper. Now ask her to spell the rhyming word LIGHT. At this point, she ought to spell it LITE. Write it down as well:

B I T E
L I T E

Let her know the second spelling ought to be correct, but this is an example of one of the trickiest spellings in English. Write the correct spelling for her:

B I T E
L I T E
L IGH T

Emphasize that while BITE is correct, LITE is not. Since the combination, IGH, represents the single sound, /I/, this is her first (and her only) example of a *three-fer*: three letters making a single sound! IGH spells long I.

Now discuss the spelling of FIGHT: should it be FITE or FIGHT? Don't keep her in suspense; let her know *nearly* all the words ending in the sound "ITE" are spelled with this new three-fer. Show her the relevant columns of words in Appendix N and let her read them. At the end of this list you can both marvel at how the words BITE, KITE, and SPITE escaped this spelling madness!

As if three-fers weren't bad enough, you and your child are now faced with some awesome *four-fers*! Do the AUGH and OUGH word groups in the appendix together because these are both alternate spellings for the same sound: /aw/. Here's what you might do with your child. Ask him to spell the word TAUGHT, as in "I taught my dog a new trick." If necessary, help him isolate the 3 sounds in this word (/t/ + /aw/ + /t/) and replace each of those sounds with appropriate letters, writing his answer on some paper. Given what you both did in Stage 13, he should end up with one of two phonetically correct alternatives:

T A U T   T A W T

Either of these is a great answer. The word TAUGHT *should* be spelled one of these 2 already-established ways. Now write the correct spelling below his:

T A U T
T A U G H T

Let him ponder this horrendous spelling for a moment. Then point out that, in the correct spelling, the 2 T's make perfect sense, but the vowel sound, /aw/, is spelled differently from what he learned in Stage 13: AUGH instead of AW or AU.

In other words, AUGH must be a *four-fer* for the sound /aw/! Tell him AUGH and OUGH are *both* alternate spellings for the vowel sound /aw/ and write some additional words for him to read:

TAUT

TAUGHT

CAUGHT

BOUGHT

FOUGHT

Let him know there are only 3 four-fers in English – and he just met 2 of them. Go to the appendix and show him both listings (AUGH and OUGH) under the GH Groups. It might be helpful to transfer these words to index cards where, initially, they could be written this way: S-OUGH-T, D-AUGH-TER, N-AUGH-TY, and so on. In each case, the middle part of the word is read as /aw/. Help with definitions of these words as necessary.

So, the sound /aw/ now has 4 correct spellings: AU, AW, AUGH, and OUGH. Compare: FAULT, LAW, TAUGHT, and SOUGHT.

You have one last four-fer and then you're done with them. Ask him if he can remember how to spell the number 8 from the Tricky 50 list in Stage 15. If he has trouble, get out the deck of cards you made for reviewing those tricky words. Now write it on a piece of paper:

EIGHT

Since EIGHT has only 2 sounds, /A/ and /t/, EIGH must be another spelling of long A. The word EIGHT is not alone in having this weird spelling. Write these words under the word EIGHT, lining them up nicely:

EIGHT

WEIGHT

WEIGH

SLEIGH

FREIGHT

Can he read all of them now? Make sure he understands the difference in meaning between the above words and ATE, WAIT, WAY, and SLAY. Now go to the appendix and see if he can figure out those 2 words that remain in this group: NEIGH and NEIGHBOR. The exception word in this group, HEIGHT, would be pronounced HATE if we used the word EIGHT as a guide. It's actual pronunciation is HITE – a spelling that would have been perfectly reasonable! Sometimes, English spelling is simply unfathomable. <u>Note</u>: Now he has 4 spellings for the sound /A/: A-E, AI, AY, and EIGH. Compare: SALE, SAIL, SLAY, and SLEIGH.

There is one last listing in the GH Groups in the appendix. The five words there all have the spelling OUGH or AUGH, yet these spellings do not say /aw/ in this group. What these 5 words *do* have in common is the fact that GH spells /f/. Just show her the listing in the appendix and explain that for these 5 words, GH is a two-fer for the sound /f/. That alone may be enough for her to identify some of them. You could also tell her they are such oddball words that you're going to spell them as they *should* have been spelled, that is, phonetically. Write this for her:

ROUGH = RUFF
TOUGH = TUFF
ENOUGH = ENUFF
LAUGH = LAFF
COUGH = CAUFF

Once she realizes what these words actually are, point out that 3 of them rhyme, and GH spells /f/ for all of them. These are some of the craziest spellings that exist in English, yet they are all common words; she needs to master them. Make up some humorous sentences for her to read – sentences that might help her remember these words:

- I'm ROUGH and I'm TOUGH but I've had ENOUGH of these silly spellings!
- These spellings make me LAUGH!
- These spellings make me want to COUGH, BURP, and TWITCH!

Note: Two other common words that would normally be covered here, THOUGH and THROUGH, will be covered in Stage 18.

Time to evaluate. When you think she has mastered all the words in the entire GH group, put the most common of these words on flash cards, shuffle them, and see how she does. This is a TOUGH test. Take your time and be sure she knows these words – they occur frequently in children's books.

After the GH groups, the PH group will be easy. Whether this two-fer is at the beginning of a word, in the middle, or at the end, it always has the sound /f/. There are some amusing words in this group that should make the task of remembering how to pronounce PH an easy one. With the substitution of F for PH, all the words are surprisingly phonetic. See how she does simply reading from the list.

I think the hardest word on the list is SPHERE. If necessary, write SFERE on a card and hide the S: FERE. Once she reads it, show the S: SFERE. Now substitute the PH for the F: SPHERE. Tell her it's just a fancy name for BALL.

Next up: some words which simply don't follow the rules! In the appendix, I call them the WILD group since WILD is one of the words listed there. All your child's experience to date would suggest the vowels in the WILD Group should have their short sound. Nevertheless, all these vowels are long. If all these words ended in E, like they once did in OLDE English, your CHILDE would FINDE MOSTE of them trivial. Even though that final E has long since vanished, he must still recognize these two dozen common words.

Simply show him the list with the caution that all the vowels are long; he shouldn't have too much trouble. Point out that the word WIND can be said with a long I, or a short I, but the meaning changes with the pronunciation. Also, point out that FROST, COST, and LOST are not on the list because they are pronounced exactly as we would expect, with a short O.

Now, focus your child's attention on a common suffix that is always pronounced in a manner at odds with its spelling: TION. (Over 4000 English words end in this suffix.) If you think about words like ACTION, FICTION, and ADDITION, it becomes apparent that TION is pronounced "SHIN" (or, perhaps, "SHUN," depending on where you live). What is most unusual in this situation is that T says /sh/. (That the vowel in this unstressed suffix is pronounced /i/ or /u/ is another example of Lazy Vowel.) In Appendix N, I have included a list of words that should get your child accustomed to reading this common word ending. The key here, is that she does *not* try to sound out this suffix phonetically; she must simply recognize it and think: SHIN. Use flash cards and go slowly; many of these words are two (or more) syllables. Define them as necessary.

Next, look at the TURE family of words in the appendix. If you think about how you pronounce words like FIXTURE and PASTURE, you can hear that TURE does not rhyme with PURE and CURE. Instead, TURE is pronounced /ch/ + /er/, or simply "CHER". With this understanding of how to read TURE, the words in this group are surprisingly phonetic. If necessary, with a word like SIGNATURE, hide the TURE part of the word and let your child read SIGNA. Then she simply needs to add the sound "CHER" to read the entire word. She'll likely need help with some definitions, even after successfully pronouncing some of these words.

In multi-syllable words, each syllable has a vowel. Often, these are stand-alone vowels that can have either their short or long sound. So now you can show your child some general strategies for deciding how to pronounce these vowels. For example, the words HABIT and BASIC are both two-syllable CVCVC words. Yet in one, the A is long, and in the other, short. Why? A related question is this: in longer words, how does the reader figure out syllable boundaries?

It turns out there are some general rules that can help a beginning reader in this regard. Here is a summary of the most helpful ones:

- *Open* syllables end in a vowel (CCV, CV, V) and typically have a long vowel sound: BA/SIC. BA is an open syllable. SIC is not.
- *Closed* syllables end in a consonant (CVC, VC) and typically have a short vowel sound: HAB/IT. Both HAB and IT are closed syllables.
- Syllable boundaries occur between consecutive consonants, if possible, for example, BUT/TER and MAS/TER. Note how this rule keeps us from reading MASTER as MA/STER. (In MA/STER, the A would have a long sound because MA is an open syllable.)
- Syllable boundaries *never* split consonant digraphs (SH, CH, TH, NG) because digraphs produce a single sound. So, the word BISHOP can't be read as BIS/HOP. However, that still leaves two possibilities: BI/SHOP (long I) or BISH/OP (short I). Here, only more reading experience can help – and the fact that BI/SHOP is not a word.
- Common prefixes (DE, DIS, EM, IM, IN, IR, MIS, NON, PRE, RE, SUB, UN) and common suffixes (ED, ER, ES, EST, ING, FUL, LESS, LY, MENT, NESS, OUS, Y) are always their own syllable and they obey the above rules for open and closed syllables.
- TION and TURE (covered above) are always their own syllable.

The above guidelines are for you. I believe, however, that your child can understand the open/closed distinction and the necessity of splitting a word at two consecutive middle consonants (unless those consonants form a two-fer).

Teacher Note: These guidelines are not perfect. A beginner trying to read words like HOTEL or COMET for the first time could still misread them as HOT/EL (short O) and CO/MET (long O). If these words are already in the beginner's *speaking* vocabulary, such mistakes will be minimized. These mistakes will also decrease with time and reading experience.

In Appendix N, the two of you will find some practice groups for reading words with open and closed syllables. Don't think your child must master all these words before moving on. There are too many. Do some now, from each group, until she gets the hang of it – and have her come back, at any time, for more practice. In the first group, the initial syllable is closed. In the second, the initial syllable is open. In the third group, you'll find a wonderful mix. Be sure she understands that for open syllables, the vowel is long, and for closed, the vowel is short.

I split the words into syllables myself so that, initially, the reading of longer words would be a little easier for your child. Naturally, she won't have this aid when she is reading independently. Nonetheless, this experience of reading words that have been divided for her will still be a useful one: her confidence will keep growing and she'll be learning to view longer words as the sum of pieces (syllables) that are individually manageable. She'll also be learning that, faced with an unknown word, multiple pronunciations are often possible. MOMENT for example, might be pronounced MOM/ENT (short O) or MO/MENT (long O). When one of the pronunciations match up with a word in her *speaking* vocabulary, she'll know which to pick.

In doing this work, I found some words to be problematic. For instance, in the appendix I did IN/VES/TIG/A/TION instead of IN/VES/TI/GA/TION. I did so to keep a short I in the 3rd syllable. Yet the second way of dividing the word seems more natural to me. Clearly, the rules I summarized above, are helpful, but fallible.

Another way to look at a word like INVESTIGATION, is to realize that the second I is in an unaccented part of the word. Therefore, it is likely to be pronounced with a short I (or short U), in line with our earlier discussion of Lazy Vowel.

Stage 17
Soft C, Soft G, Contractions

This is the last stage before you turn your child loose for a lifetime of independent reading and self-directed learning. The topics you'll investigate with him include:

- The vowel Y in the middle of a word: what is its sound?
- Alternate sounds for some consonants. Your child has already seen that S can spell /z/. But in addition, C can spell /s/ (CITY), and G can spell /j/ (GENTLE). What rules govern this behavior?
- Contractions. As soon as your child opens a book, he'll run into words like DON'T and HAVEN'T. You need to teach him what these are and how to pronounce them.
- Thousands of words end in E. When is that E silent? What does the silent E tell him about the word to which it is attached?
- The vowel digraphs IE and EI – how should he handle these two-fers? What sounds do they symbolize?

The Spelling Corner – Stage 16 words are not easy words to spell. Do what you can, but realize that your child has years to work on her spelling. It might be best to start with words from the WILD group in Appendix N: they are common words with relatively easy spellings. Next, see how she does with some of the easier words in the GIGGLE group – words like APPLE, BOTTLE, and NOODLE.

If you ask her to spell some of the words from the GH group, remind her that these are among the trickiest spellings in the English language. She should expect the three-fer, IGH, and the four-fers AUGH, OUGH, and EIGH. See how she does with one of these words, NIGHT, for instance, and once she gets it, stay with other words that rhyme with NIGHT. If she hears a word ending in "SHIN," does she remember to spell it as TION? Explain to her that nearly every word having the sound /f/ is spelled with F, not PH. She should use PH only if she is sure that PH is the correct spelling.

Ask her to spell some of the multi-syllable words as well. Clearly pronounce each syllable so she can hear whether the syllable is open or closed.

The two of you have already investigated the letter Y when it occurs at the beginning of a word as a consonant (Stage 7), and at the end of a word as a vowel (Stages 13 and 14). If Y appears in the middle of a word or syllable, it should be read as a vowel having the sound /I/ or /i/. Look at the two word groups I have prepared in Appendix O. In one group, the Y spells long I; in the other, short I.

Both groups nearly perfectly follow the rules for open and closed syllables. Tell your child you want her to find the 3 animals that are in these combined two groups (PYTHON, HYENA, LYNX). If she imagines each Y as the letter I, the words in both groups are surprisingly phonetic. Help with syllable boundaries (if needed) by writing them out for her. For example:

ty/phoon symp/tom
an/al/yze hyp/no/tize

If she has trouble with LYNX, simply rewrite it as LINKS. It's perfectly phonetic. LYNX = LINKS = /l/ + /i/ + /ng/ + /k/ + /s/.

Your child has already seen how to use S (or ES) to form the plural. She has also seen that it's common for S to have a Z sound. In Appendix O, I have a group of common words that have nothing to do with the plural, yet the S sounds like a Z. Make sure she can read and pronounce these words correctly.

The letter C symbolizes two primary sounds, neither unique, but both important. When C is followed by A, O, or U, it has a K sound. You already covered this with your child in Stage 4. However, when C is followed by E, I, or Y, it has an S sound. "Hard C" refers to its K sound, while "Soft C" refers to its S sound. In Appendix O, I have included some of the more common words where a soft C is required. There are no exceptions to this soft C rule: CE, CI, and CY should all be pronounced as though they were written as SE, SI, and SY:

CENTER = SENTER   CITY = SITY   CYNIC = SINIC

Happily, this rule makes hundreds of additional words 100% phonetic.

After explaining to your child when a soft C is required, show him the appropriate group in the appendix. Initially, the words rhyme, but not for long. If necessary, replace the C with an S in some of the words (EX/SEPT) as a temporary reading aid. Point out to him that the silent E in a word like BOUNCE has nothing to do with making a prior vowel long. It is there solely to make the C soft.

There is a parallel situation with the letter G. G has its "hard" sound, /g/, when it is followed by A, O, or U. Its "soft" sound, /j/, occurs when G is followed by E, I, or Y. In Appendix O, you'll find a sampling of such words. In this case, there *are* some common exceptions to the rule. I included them at the end of the list. Here are some things to note as the two of you work through this soft G list:

- The silent E in a word like CAGE serves two functions: it makes the A long and the G soft.
- The silent E in a word like PLEDGE is there only to make the G soft. The other E has its short sound.
- In the word, ORANGE, the NG is not a two-fer. The word needs to be read in a way that interprets GE as a unit rather than NG. Orange = /or/ + /i/ + /n/ + /j/. Lazy Vowel is at work in the second syllable.
- There are other Lazy Vowel examples in this list: ORIGINAL, GENERAL, and even the word SAUSAGE (/s/ + /aw/ + /s/ + /i/ + /j/).
- The word GIRL is only an apparent exception to the soft G rule. The letter I in this word is an inseparable part of the two-fer IR. As such, it should *not* change the pronunciation of the G from hard to soft. Still, the spelling, GURL, would have been a more logical choice.
- Many words like FINGER, ANGER, HUNGER, and LONGER are *not* among the exceptions because both NG and ER are inseparable two-fers in such words. The E in these words has no effect on the G; instead, it's an integral part of the R: ER = /er/.

Once again, you can temporarily replace the G with a J if it helps him to read some of these words: MA/JIC, JI/GAN/TIC. Soft C and soft G occur frequently in English. Once you and your child finish this section, he'll be able to decode hundreds of additional words.

Countless English words end in the single vowel E. I estimate a final E is silent 99% of the time. Your child already knows most of the important exceptions to this rule, namely, the one-syllable words in the E/EE group from Appendix G: ME, WE, SHE, HE, THE, and so on. Apart from these few exceptions, final E's are nearly always silent. Think of how useful this rule is for the beginning reader. Up until this stage, you have deliberately given her the impression that silent E has only one purpose: to make the other vowel in the syllable long. In this current stage, you have expanded the role of a final, silent E: attached to a C or a G, final E causes a "soft" sound.

If you look in the appendix, you'll see there are some additional roles of silent E. I have 9 categories there, labeled A through I, with examples in each category. The category descriptions are given below. The goal here is to teach your child that a silent E at the end of a word can have many meanings. The categories in the appendix are as follows:

A) The E makes the prior vowel in the syllable long. This is the most important, and the most common, role of a final E.
B) The E makes the prior C soft. It may, or may not, also make the prior vowel long.

C) The E makes the prior G soft. It may, or may not, also make the prior vowel long.

D) All English syllables must have a vowel.

E) English words don't end in V.

F) English Words don't end in U. (The main exceptions are MENU, TOFU, FLU, GURU, and, of course, YOU.)

G) Nouns that are singular, yet end in S, could cause confusion. A final E announces that the word is singular and it prepares the word for the second S that will make it plural (HOUSE/HOUSES).

H) Some words end in E for no apparent reason whatsoever! Your child has already seen many of these listed as tricky words.

I) Worse still, in some words, a final E is utterly misleading as to how the word should be pronounced: it would seem to indicate a long vowel when, in fact, the vowel stays short. Notice: these are all examples of Lazy Vowel.

Beginning readers should be aware of categories A through F. I recommend that a teacher cover the final 3 categories only with older students and adults. As always, use your own judgment. I suggest you simply explain each category and let your child read the words. It provides good review, and it shows her that a final, silent E has multiple uses.

Next up are the two-fers IE and EI. I have postponed these until now because many EI words (like RECEIVE) use the soft C sound you just introduced to your child. Here's a pleasant fact about these two digraphs: with few exceptions, they both symbolize /E/. Look at the lists I've provided in the appendix. Note how consistently the sound of both EI and IE is long E. This is another useful rule for the beginning reader. You have already covered nearly all the exceptions to this rule:

- the EIGH group from Appendix N: EIGHT, WEIGHT, SLEIGH, and so on
- the small, IE group from Appendix M: TIE, DIE, LIE, and PIE

Of the other exception words listed in Appendix O, FRIEND and THEIR are the most important. Ask your child how FRIEND ought to be spelled (FREND).

As you help your child read these words, point out to him how many have a soft C sound, and how many end in silent E simply to keep the word from ending in V. Note that the E at the end of HYGIENE and CAFFEINE serves no purpose whatever, and that for the rhyming words, SHRIEK and SHEIK, one uses IE and the other uses EI.

It's time to deal, formally, with contractions. They pop up everywhere so it's a good idea to cover them here or they will confuse and frustrate your child as he sets out on his own in Stage 18. I have 33 of the *most common* contractions listed in Appendix O. (There are nearly 100 contractions in English, but many of them are obscure, MIGHT'VE, for example.) To motivate this topic with your child, get a piece of paper and write:

He is eating.

She is sleeping.

We are playing.

Have him read these 3 simple sentences. Now, focusing on the first sentence, have him read it repeatedly, but each time a little faster. As he does so, can he hear how the two words, HE and IS, start coming together? Explain that, when we speak, we often say: "He's eating" instead of "He is eating".

Now write "He's eating" across from "He is eating." on the above paper:

He is eating.   He's eating.

She is sleeping.

We are playing.

Let him study it for a while; this is a novel (and weird) topic for him. Point out that HE'S is called a *contraction*: a combination of two words into one. A contraction is a short-cut method of both speaking and writing – and such contractions are everywhere. Point out how the word IS is *partially* gone. The S is still there, but something called an *apostrophe* has taken the place of the missing I. Also, point out that the original sentence has 4 syllables while the short-cut sentence has only three. If spelled like it sounds, we would write HE'S as HEEZ. Make sure he understands this equivalency:

He's   =   He is

Show him this contraction in Appendix O and tell him "Only 32 more!" (Don't worry! They'll start going faster as he gets the hang of it!)

Now, do the same thing as above with the other two short sentences. As you do so, make these points:

- SHE'S, sounds like SHEEZ, and it's short for SHE IS. The apostrophe again takes the place of I in this example.
- WE'RE, sounds like WEER, and it's short for WE ARE. The apostrophe takes the place of A in this example.

When finished, your paper will look like this:

He is eating.   He's eating.

She is sleeping.   She's sleeping.

We are playing.   We're playing.

Can he read all six sentences correctly? Now, let him help you make 3 flash cards – one for each contraction above. On one side, write the contraction (SHE'S, for instance) and on the other, write what it's short for (SHE IS).

Before moving on, point out how awesome are the new words he's just learned: CONTRACTION and APOSTROPHE. Both words are perfectly phonetic given the phonics and rules we have already discussed – including the interpretation of open and closed syllables.

Ok, that was an elaborate introduction to three of the contractions listed in the appendix. Now you can speed things up a bit. There are 7 contractions that involve the word WILL. Write out these 6 short sentences on paper:

I will go with you.

You will go with me.

He will go with us.

She will go with us.

They will go with us.

We will go with them.

Have her read them and then tell her that the first two words in each sentence have a single-syllable contraction. Can she guess what any of them might be? One at a time, go back and write the same sentence, but with the contraction, each time emphasizing the correct pronunciation. (I would include the phonetic pronunciation in the parentheses.)

I will go with you.   I'll go with you. (ILE)

You will go with me.   You'll go with me. (YOOL)

He will go with us.   He'll go with us. (HEEL)

She will go with us.   She'll go with us. (SHEEL)

They will go with us.   They'll go with us. (THAIL)

We will go with them.   We'll go with them. (WEEL)

Let her read each sentence on her own while you monitor her pronunciation. Does she see that the apostrophe takes the place of WI in each case?

Now ask her this: what if everyone in these 6 sentences wanted to stay home? In other words, how would we *negate* these 6 sentences? See if you can lead her to the correct contraction, WON'T (will not). The correct pronunciation is WOANT.

I will go with you.	I'll go with you.	I won't go with you.
You will go with me.	You'll go with me.	You won't go with me.
He will go with us.	He'll go with us.	He won't go with us.
She will go with us.	She'll go with us.	She won't go with us.
They will go with us.	They'll go with us.	They won't go with us.
We will go with them.	We'll go with them.	We won't go with them.

Now make 7 new flash cards to go with the 3 you made earlier.

_____

Now that your child knows contractions can be used to negate things, you can do the other 13 negating contractions as a large group. (I leave it to you to decide whether to include the slang contraction AIN'T for AM NOT. AIN'T is perfectly phonetic, and it rhymes with PAINT.)

She <u>is not</u> going with us.

He <u>can not</u> go with us.

I <u>do not</u> want to go.

She <u>does not</u> want to go.

We <u>are not</u> going!

She <u>could not</u> go.

He <u>would not</u> go.

I <u>should not</u> eat so fast!

We <u>did not</u> sleep well.

I <u>have not</u> seen her today.

He <u>has not</u> had his bath yet.

She <u>was not</u> home.

They <u>were not</u> sleepy.

Make it a game. Underline the two words that will get a contraction and see if he can guess what that contraction might be. After all, he probably uses many of these contractions in his speech already.

She <u>is not</u> going with us.	She isn't going with us. (IZINT)
He <u>cannot</u> go with us.	He can't go with us. (CANT)
I <u>do not</u> want to go.	I don't want to go. (DOANT)
She <u>does not</u> want to go.	She doesn't want to go. (DUZINT)
We <u>are not</u> going!	We aren't going! (ARNT)
She <u>could not</u> go.	She couldn't go. (COODINT)
He <u>would not</u> go.	He wouldn't go. (WOODINT)
I <u>should not</u> eat so fast!	I shouldn't eat so fast! (SHOODINT)
We <u>did not</u> swim today.	We didn't swim today. (DIDINT)
I <u>have not</u> seen her today.	I haven't seen her today. (HAVINT)
He <u>has not</u> had his bath yet.	He hasn't had his bath yet. (HAZINT)
She <u>was not</u> home.	She wasn't home. (WUZINT)
They <u>were not</u> sleepy.	They weren't sleepy. (WERNT)

Make up 13 more flash cards and take a well-deserved break.

Do the last 10 contractions as a group, as you did above. By the *end* of this final exercise, your paper will look like something like this:

<u>Let us</u> go to the game today!	Let's go to the game today! (LETZ)
<u>I am</u> not sleepy yet!	I'm not sleepy yet! (IME)
<u>It is</u> not polite to pick your nose.	It's not polite… (ITS)
<u>He is</u> here! <u>I have</u> seen him!	He's here! I've seen him! (IVE)
<u>They are</u> coming to the game.	They're coming… (THAIR)
<u>They have</u> had enough!	They've had enough! (THAVE)
<u>Who is</u> that lady in the blue dress?	Who's that lady… (HOOZ)
<u>We have</u> had a great time today!	We've had a great… (WEEV)
<u>You are</u> my best friend!	You're my best friend! (YOOR)
<u>You have</u> been a big help today!	You've been a big… (YOOV)

Make up your final 10 flash cards and add them to the deck. For the next few days, review all 33 contractions using the flash cards. When you practice with your child, show her one side, and have her predict the other (in both directions). Make sure she is pronouncing the contraction correctly. Once you are convinced she knows them, it's time to move on to the last stage in this reading program.

Stage 18
Independent Reading

Certainly, congratulations are in order! Look how far you've traveled with your child. Remember back in Stage 2 when you pointed to the letters in MOM for a couple seconds each, showing him how to blend his first word? Now he has all the skills he needs to begin reading independently. You've given him an invaluable gift, one he can repay only if he, at some point in the future, teaches someone else to read, as you have done for him.

Your child deserves accolades as well. He has successfully completed a challenging project and, whatever his age, he has become a "reader." His independent reading will be hesitant at first, but he will quickly gain in speed, confidence, vocabulary, and fluency. He now has the crucial ability not only to self-entertain, but to *self-teach.* New worlds, real and imaginary, are open to him for exploration whenever he wants. This stage marks his transition from "learning to read" to "reading to learn."

Stage 18, then, is different from the previous stages. For one, this stage never really ends. For another, your role now shifts: you will be less his teacher, and more his monitor and his coach. If you look at appendices P and Q, you'll see you've already taught him about 95% of the code that is there. You'll present the final 5% during this stage, but at a more leisurely pace, when these final topics come up naturally in the course of his independent reading. Daily, formal instruction is no longer a requirement. What he needs now, more than anything else, is to read – but in a *supervised* setting.

So, take a break from formal instruction for a while. There are still some topics to teach (see "Completing the Code" below) but you can tie up these "loose ends" during the next few months, as he becomes a more fluent reader. Here are my recommendations for the *immediate* future:

- Get a good dictionary – perhaps one specifically designed for beginning readers. Show her how to use it by searching for some words she already knows.
- Go to a library and let her pick out lots of age-appropriate books. I wouldn't worry too much about whether books are at the "right" level. If a book is too easy for her, or too difficult, she'll quickly get bored and put it down. Within reason, allow her to be the judge.
- For a significant time, you want her to read *out loud*, in your presence. This allows you to monitor her reading and to see if there are any

unexpected problem areas. Find a balance between intervening too fast, in order to help, and allowing her to become frustrated. If a book is clearly too difficult for her, help her switch to one that will allow her more success.

As you listen to her read, be aware there are at least five ways things can (and will) go wrong:

1) She reads a word incorrectly because she forgets something she has already learned: that AI says /A/, for example, or that GE says /j/ or that SAID is one of the Tricky Words, so it doesn't rhyme with MAID.
2) She reads a word phonetically, but nonetheless incorrectly, because the word does not follow standard phonics rules: BALLET, CHOIR, COLONEL.
3) She accents the wrong syllable: CON/ceal rather than con/CEAL.
4) She divides a multi-syllable word incorrectly: BON/US (/o/) instead of BO/NUS (/O/).
5) She pronounces a word correctly but it's not in her speaking or listening vocabulary, so she misses the main idea of the sentence.

Deal directly with situation #1 (above) by reviewing with her whatever phonics she has forgotten. If, for example, she reads DEAD incorrectly, as DEED, remind her that DEAD is one of the exception words in Appendix K. If the word were BEAD or PLEAD, her pronunciation would be correct. Also, it's unlikely the word DEED will make sense in the context of the sentence if the actual word is DEAD.

Situation #2 is more problematic. Tell her she is correct with her phonics but CHOIR, for example, is one of those words in English that doesn't follow the rules. See if she can correct herself, by looking at the word within the context of the sentence. If that doesn't work, encourage her to look it up in a dictionary. This is preferable to simply telling her what the word is, for two reasons. Looking up CHOIR will reinforce its odd spelling. It will also encourage her to be less dependent upon you. I find it's a good exercise to ask, once the word is identified, how the word should have been spelled in order to be considered phonetic: QUIRE (or KWIRE)

There is no quick fix for situations #3 and #4. These types of mistakes will naturally decrease over time as her reading fluency and vocabulary grow. Take the opportunity to remind her that English is an accented language, meaning that in multi-syllable words, one syllable is usually spoken more forcibly than the others. Go back with her to the longer words in Appendix N and have her re-read some of them with this accenting in mind. Show her there are some words that she can accent either way, but the meaning changes with the accenting:

OB / ject   or   ob / JECT
REB / el   or   re / BEL
PER / mit   or   per / MIT

Situation #5 is a learning opportunity. Tell her one of the many reasons for reading is to increase her vocabulary. As in situation #2, she should first try to figure out what the correctly-decoded word might mean from its context. Then she should consult a dictionary to see if her contextual guess is correct. At a minimum, she should ask you what the decoded word means. Remind her *never* to skip a word she doesn't know.

Continue reading *to* him on a regular basis even though he is now reading books on his own. Most children will still enjoy this. You'll find he follows the text avidly as you read. Stop to point out unusual, rule-breaking words. Note with him how often the 50 Tricky Words show up.

Encourage him to write if his motor skills allow it. If he is still quite young, you can spend some time with him practicing and drawing individual letters. Encourage him to write notes to you (which you can reciprocate), little stories, descriptions of things that happen to him – anything to keep improving his spelling skills.

Familiarize yourself with the phonics topics remaining (see below) so that if one of those topics comes up naturally while he is reading, you can cover the topic at that time. The topic most likely to come up first is the one I call "Other Vowel Combinations."

At some point (don't rush this!) your child will be ready to start reading quietly – "reading in my brain," as my daughter called it. If your child is young, don't assume he knows what this is. All his life, his experience of reading has been listening to you read and, more recently, reading aloud himself. My three-year-old daughter, an independent reader at the time, one morning asked my wife and me why we were staring at the newspaper for so long. We then realized she had no idea we were reading. I relate this story only to alert you that you may have to coach your son in this regard. Simply tell him reading silently is possible – he'll figure it out.

Once silent reading begins, regularly remind him not to simply skip over words he doesn't know. Encourage him to use the dictionary or to ask you for help. You may also want to show him that he can type a word whose meaning is unknown, LOLLYGAG, for instance, into an internet search window to get an online definition: "fool around, dawdle." When he finishes his silent reading of a book, get him to talk about it, so you can gauge his comprehension.

Completing the Code

The 50 Irregular Words of English

If you look at Appendix S, you'll find my *final* version of the Tricky 50 irregular English words. I know what you're thinking. Wasn't that the final version you saw back in Stage 15? Well, I did remark at the time that the words HER, OUR, MY, GO, and SAY had become wholly phonetic. Rather than simply take these five words off the list, making it the Tricky 45, I think it more helpful to replace them with 5 relatively important words that are definitely *not* phonetic: EYE, WATER, FRIEND, THOUGH, and THROUGH.

I leave it to you to introduce these 5 new tricky words to your child and to add 5 new cards to the deck you used for practice in Stage 15. Use the full deck once a week to keep reviewing these 50 high-frequency words until he knows all of them cold.

Other Vowel Combinations

If you look back at the vowel digraphs (two-fers) you covered in the previous stages, you'll find these: AI, EE, EA, OA, OO, UE, OI, OU, AU, OE, IE, and EI. Each of these produces a single sound. There are, however, other vowel combinations. I don't mean AA, II, UU, AE, and AO – no common words have these spellings. But that still leaves EU, IO, EO, IU, UI, UA, and IA. Only one in this last group, EU, is a digraph. If you look at Appendix T, you'll see it's an uncommon two-fer in English. Its sound is either /y/ + /ew/ or /ew/. Those 11 words are all I could find and none of them are likely to show up in a child's book. My advice is to skip this group entirely with a young child, but to cover it with a school-age child or an adult.

The key thing to understand about the other 6 new vowel combinations (IO, EO, IU, UI, UA, and IA) is they are *not* two-fers. This implies *both* letters make a sound, and therefore a syllable boundary occurs between each of these pairs of vowels. This will be something new for your child. The two of you can look together at these 6 groupings in Appendix T.

Discuss the IO group first. Since a syllable boundary occurs between the I and the O, the I will be in an open syllable. Your child should therefore expect a long vowel sound and that's what she will get: either long I or long E. The O will be long or short, depending on whether it's in an open or closed syllable. There are some common words here. I didn't include any words ending in TION because that's the special sound ("SHIN") you already covered in Stage 16. There are many words that end in IOUS as well, but you'll cover those in the OUS group further below. The main point to stress here is that IO is not a two-fer – so both vowels make a sound.

There are no surprises in the EO group: both letters make a sound and the E is long. In a few of the words, like DUNGEON for example, the 2 sounds of EO nearly merge into what sounds like a short I: DUN / GIN. This is another example of Lazy Vowel. As expected, the G in DUNGEON has its soft sound.

In the IU group, I have included only a small sampling of the hundreds of words that end in IUM. The letter I has a long E sound in an open syllable while the U is short because it's in a syllable closed by the M. Be aware of the soft C in CALCIUM and the soft G in GERANIUM.

Let's discuss the next 2 groups together: UA and UI. I have eliminated from these groups, words like QUAKE and QUIT where the U is an integral part of the Q, making the side-by-side vowel structure only apparent. With Q words accounted for earlier, the UA group is perfectly well-behaved. U has its long sound, /y/ + /ew/, or, in some cases, simply /ew/. In the words spelled with AL, the AL has the lazy ULL sound you and your child first saw in Stage 14. In TRUANT and in LANGUAGE the final vowel defaults to a lazy /i/:

$$/t/ + /r/ + /ew/ + /i/ + /n/ + /t/$$
$$/l/ + /a/ + /ng/ + /g/ + /w/ + /i/ + /j/.$$

In the UI group, the words in the first box are what the 2 of you might expect at this point. There are few common UI words. In the second boxed group (FRUIT, JUICE and others), you see yet another (infrequent) spelling of the sound /ew/. For these 6 words, UI *is* acting as a two-fer, producing a single sound. We may prefer the spelling FROOT JOOSE, but we must deal with the language we have! In the third boxed group of UI words, the U is silent. It's there simply to keep the G from going "soft." The word GUESS, for instance, without that silent U (GESS) would have to be pronounced JESS, as in DIGEST. Cool, right? There are few words where this phenomenon occurs.

The entire IA group is what you would both expect: a long vowel sound (E or I) on the open side of the syllable divide, and a short vowel sound on the closed. The words listed are only a small sampling of such words. Note: for words *ending* in IA, the sound of the A defaults to a lazy /u/.

Past Tense Can Be Tricky

Take a few moments to remind your child that a verb is the action word in a sentence – the word describing what the person, animal, or thing is doing:

I <u>snore</u> when I <u>sleep</u>.   He <u>plays</u> with his brother.
She <u>kisses</u> her dad.   The flower <u>wilts</u> in the sun.

Sometimes, the action occurs in the past (yesterday). To indicate the past, we usually add D or ED to regular verbs:

I <u>snored</u> last night.   He <u>played</u> with his brother last week.
She <u>kissed</u> her dad.   The flower <u>wilted</u> in the heat.

The following rules for adding D or ED are complex. They are for you, not for your child.

- If the verb already ends in E, simply add the D (LOVE, LOVED)
- If the verb has a vowel digraph (OA, EE, AW, and so on), simply add ED (CHEER, CHEERED)
- If the verb has a single vowel followed by a single consonant, double the final consonant and add ED (WAG, WAGGED).
- If the verb ends in the sound /sh/, /ch/, /s/, /k/, /p/, or /f/, the added D or ED will have a /t/ sound (KISS/KISSED, NURSE/NURSED.
- If the verb ends with a /d/ or a /t/ sound, adding D or ED will create a second syllable (FLOAT, FLOATED).
- If the verb ends in the single vowel Y, change the Y to I and add ED (MARRY, MARRIED).

Rather than expect your child to remember all this (she won't), have her look in Appendix T where I have examples of each of the above 6 situations. You can choose whether to explain why each group happens as it does. I would simply have her practice each group separately, helping her with pronunciation, and making sure each past tense verb remains a single syllable (except when it doesn't!)

Comparative and Superlative

The rules for forming comparative and superlative are similar to the above rules for forming past tense – especially for when to double the consonant. Here, too, we change Y to I before adding ER or EST.

fat – fatter – fattest
sweet – sweeter – sweetest
rainy – rainier – rainiest

First, give her a concrete example: we use a word without a special ending, TALL for instance, to describe a single child: Dave is a mighty *tall* dude! We add the ending ER to compare two children: Dave is *taller* than Sheila. And we add the ending EST to compare 3 or more children: Dave is the *tallest* kid in his class.

Sum it up for her: when describing a single noun (person, place, thing) use *neither* ER nor EST; when comparing two nouns, use the ending ER; when comparing 3 or more nouns, use the ending EST. Once she understands the concept, let her read the triplets I've provided in the appendix.

Additional Word Families

Look in the appendix at the -OUS, -SION, -SURE, -CIAL, and -TIAL families. Many of these words in these families will be unfamiliar to a young child even though he may well be able to accurately pronounce them. You may want to choose what to cover here. Certainly, with an adult or an older child, I would cover all these groups.

With a preschooler, I would teach the equivalency of the spelling, OUS, with the sound "ISS." Then I would have her look only at those words in the OUS group that she likely already knows (such as JOYOUS, NERVOUS, FAMOUS, FABULOUS, DANGEROUS, and GENEROUS). Of course, you can spend some time here teaching new vocabulary as well. Note that in all these words, Lazy Vowel is causing the final vowel sound to degenerate to "ISS."

In the IOUS group, I would again restrict the words if I were teaching a preschooler: CURIOUS, SERIOUS, HILARIOUS, and FURIOUS. I would omit the UOUS and the CIOUS groups entirely with a preschooler. With an older student, point out how, in all 4 of the OUS subgroups, OUS consistently says "ISS" due to the Lazy Vowel phenomenon.

In the *first* SION group, SION says "SHIN." As you recall, that is identical to the sound of TION in Stage 16. (Compare: ACTION and MISSION.) However, in the *second* SION group, as well as in the SURE group, the two of you finally encounter the 41st and final elemental sound of English. That sound is *voiced* SH, symbolically, /SH/. I first mentioned this unusual sound back in Chapter 2. It can clearly be heard in the word ASIA: /A/ + /SH/ + /u/. Even though it is the *voiced* equivalent of /sh/, it is never spelled SH. If you look over the 2 groups of words with asterisks in the appendix, you'll notice this sound occurs in such common words as PLEASURE and DECISION.

In doing these voiced SH groups with your child, I wouldn't make a big deal about this voiced/unvoiced distinction. Help with the correct pronunciation. Even if she says all the SION words using the *unvoiced* version of SH (this would be correct in MISSION, but incorrect in VISION), she'll not be far off in her pronunciation of VISION. When you show her the SURE group in the appendix, remind her that the word SURE was just covered as a tricky word in Stage 15. As a stand-alone word, the S in SURE says /sh/. For this group of words, S says /SH/ – simply demonstrate for her how to give /sh/ a little voicing!

In the final two groups, CIAL and TIAL are both spellings for the same sound: "SHULL." Think of the word DULL and then replace D with SH: SHULL. All the words in these final two groups can be pronounced with the final syllable, "SHULL." In other words, the final vowel sound in all of these words is none other than our friend, Lazy Vowel: /u/. What is unusual in these two groups is that in the one, C says /sh/, and in the other, T says /sh/. With your child, simply have him equate both CIAL and TIAL with "SHULL."

The Mute Group

You've arrived at the last phonics topic in this book. What better (and easier) way to end than with the Mute Group! Here, gathered at the end of Appendix T, are some of the weirdest spellings in the English language. Happily, the number of words is quite manageable. Eleven small groups, each having a letter that simply shouldn't be there: a letter that is mute. Two of the groups, K and W, provide review, but the other 9 are new. Have fun with these words. Show them to your child and see if he can simply read them once he sees the COLUMN heading and realizes which letter is silent.

THE END...

... of Systematic Phonics
... of the Phonetic Code
... of this Reading Program

I hope you'll use this book again!
Your feedback would be much appreciated.

You can contact me at:
stephenparker81451@gmail.com

Thank you.

Appendix A

The 60 "words" that can be formed from the letters A, E, I, O, U, M, N, and S.

Boldface indicates a real word, a person's name, a prefix, or a suffix.

<u>Note</u>: In these early stages, we are treating English as though it has no irregularities. Therefore, be careful with the words SON, IS, and AS. These are irregular words in English. At this early point in the program, they should be pronounced as they are in the words <u>SON</u>IC, H<u>ISS</u>, and <u>AS</u>TEROID.

Word	Example	Word	Example	Word	Example	Word	Example
mass	mascot	**sass**	sassy	nas	nasty	as	asteroid
mess	message	ses	sesame	**-ness**	nest	**es**	escape
miss	mistake	**sis**	sister	nis	tennis	is	hiss
moss	mosquito	sos	isosceles	nos	nostril	os	ostrich
muss	musty	sus	suspense	nus	bonus	**us**	plus
mam	mammal	**Sam**	sample	nam	dynamic	**am**	amuse
mem	member	sem	seminar	nem	nemesis	**em**	empty
mim	mimic	**sim**	simple	nim	nimble	im	improve
mom	mommy	som	somber	nom	nominate	om	omelet
mum	mumble	**sum**	summer	num	number	um	umbrella
man	manage	san	sandal	**Nan**	banana	**an**	antique
men	mention	sen	sentry	nen	linen	**en**	enjoy
min	minimum	**sin**	sincere	nin	melatonin	**in**	insect
mon	monsoon	son	sonic	**non-**	nonsense	**on**	moron
mun	munch	**sun**	sunset	**nun**	enunciate	**un-**	unwrap

Appendix B

VC stands for vowel-sound/consonant-sound.
CVC stands for consonant-sound/vowel-sound/consonant-sound.

VC	CVC						
	PT	PG	PN	TG	TM	DG	DN
up	pat	peg	pan	tag	Tim	dig	Dan
at	pet	pig	pen	tug	Tom	dog	den
it	pit	gap	pin	get	mat	dug	Don
add *	pot		pun	got	met	God	Ned
Ed	putt *	PS	nap	gut	mitt *		nod
id	tap	pass *	nip		mutt *	DS	
odd *	tip	pus		TS		sad	GS
egg *	top	sap	TD	toss *	TN	Sid	sag
ug!		sip	tad	sat	tan	sod	gas
	PD	sup	Ted	set	ten		Gus
	pad		Todd *	sit	tin	DM	
	pod		dot		net	dam	GM
	dip	PM		GN	not	dim	mug
		Pam	PP	gun	nut	mad	gum
	DD	map	pap	nag		mid	
	dad	mop	pep	nog +	TT	mud	
	did		pip		tot		
	dud		pop	GG			
			pup	gag			
				gig			

* These words are still considered CVC (or VC) because double consonants like SS, TT, and DD make a single sound. Double consonants are not blends.
+ Technically not a word but you can combine it with EGG and she'll have her first two-syllable word!

<u>Note</u>: Boxed words are important, high-frequency words.

Consonant Blends

CCVC stands for a word with a *beginning* consonant blend.
CVCC has a *final* consonant blend.

CCVC and CVCC				CCVCC
ST-	**SN-**	**-MP**	**-NT**	
stem	snap	imp	ant	stamp
Stan	snip	ump	mint	stomp
stun	snit	sump	pant	stump
step	snot	pomp	punt	stand
stop	snag	pump	tent	stunt
stud	snug	temp	tint	spend
		damp	dent	spent
SM-	**-ST**	dump	sent	
smug	mast	tamp		
smog	mist			
	must			
SP-	nest	**-ND**	**-PT**	
span	past	and	apt	
spin	pest	sand	opt	**CVCCC**
spun	test	end		tempt
spat	dust	send	**-SP**	
spit	gust	mend	gasp	
spot		pond		
sped		tend		

Appendix C

VC	CVC							
	BF	BT	BG	BN	FG	KP	KD	KM
ebb	buff *	bat	bag	ban	fig	cap	kid	Kim
if	fib	bet	beg	Ben	fog	cop	cod	Mack
off		bit	big	bin	gaff *	cup	cud	mock
ick!	KB	but	bug	bun	guff *	pack	deck	muck
ack!	back *	tab	gab	nab		pick *	Dick	Mick
	buck	tub		nub		peck	dock *	
	cab		BS		FS	puck	duck *	KN
	cob	BD	bass	FP	fuss			can
	cub	bad	Bess	puff		KT	KS	kin
		bed	boss		FN	cat	kiss	nick
	BP	bid	bus	FT	fan	kit	cuss	neck *
	bop	bud	sob	fat	fin	cot	sack	con
	pub	dab	sub	fit	fun	cut	sick	
		Deb				tack	sock *	
	KF		BM	FM	FD	tick	suck	KG
	cuff *	BB	bam!	fem	fad	tock		keg
		Bob	bum	miff *	fed	tuck	KK	cog
		bib	mob	muff *	doff *		kick	

* Words ending in FF or CK are CVC words because both FF and CK make a single consonant sound.

Note: Boxed words are important, high-frequency words.

CCVC and CVCC					CCVCC
ST-	SC-/SK-	SM-	-SK	-PT	scamp
stab	scab	smack	bask	kept	skimp
stub	skiff	smock	task		scant
staff	scoff		tusk	-CT	
stiff	skip		desk	act	
stuff	scat	-ST	disk	fact	
stack	skit	best	dusk	pact	
stick	scam	bust	mask	tact	
stock	skim	fast	ask		
stuck	scum	fest		-FT	
	scan	fist	-SP	aft	
SP-	skin	cast	cusp	gift	
speck	skid	cost		daft	
			-ND	deft	
-NT	SN-	-MP	band	sift	
bent	snob	bump	bend	soft	
bunt	snub	camp	bond		
font	sniff		fond		
cant *	snack		fund		

* Contractions, with proper apostrophes, will be covered in Stage 17

Appendix D

VC	CVC		Consonant Blends					
ill	LP	LD	still	lend	flab	slap	elm	clasp
Al	lap	lad	spell	lint	fluff	slip	helm	clamp
	lip	led	spill	left	flack	slop	kelp	cleft
LL	lop	lid	smell	lift	fleck	slit	gulp	flint
lull	pal	doll	skill	loft	flick	slot	pulp	clump
	pill	dull	skull		flock	sled	milk	flask
LG				blab	flag	slid	sulk	gland
lag	LF	LM	last	blob	flap	slam	silk	glint
leg	fell	Mel	list	bluff	flip	slim	film	plump
log	fill	mill	lost	black	flop	slum	pelt	plant
lug		mull	lust	block	flat	split	silt	slump
gal	LK		lisp	bled	fled			slant
gill	lack	LN	lamp	blog	floss	pluck	melt	slept
gull	lick	Nell	limp	blip		plug	felt	splint *
	lock	null	lump	blot	slab	plop!	belt	elk
LB	luck	nil	land	bless	slob	plot	tilt	Clint
lab	kill			bliss	slack	plod	self	splat!
lob			club	blam!	slick	plus	elf	spilt
bell	LS		cliff		slug	plan	cult	
bill	lass		click	clot			golf	
	less		clock	clad	glib	bland	gulf	
LT	loss		cluck	class	glob	blend		
let	sell		clog	clam	glop	blond		
lit	sill		clap	clan	glut	blast		
lot			clip		glad	blest		
tell					glass	blimp		
till					glum	blunt		

* A CCCVCC word

Appendix E

CVC		Consonant Blends					
rib	ram	brass	drug	grid	scram	rest	crest
rob	rim	brim	drum	grab	scrap	rust	crust
rub	rum	bran	drat!	grub	scrub	rasp	crisp
ref	ran	brat	dress	gruff	scrod	ramp	cramp
rack	Ron	Brad	drip	Greg	stress	romp	crimp
Rick	run	bred	drop	grill	strap	rump	crump
rock	rat	brick	drab	grass	strip	rant	crept
rag	rot	brag	drag	grin	struck	runt	craft
rig	rut			grim		rent	
rug	red	crass	Fran	grip	frost	rend	primp
rap	rid	cross	fret	grit	frump	rapt	prompt
rip	rod	cram	Fred	grad	frisk	risk	print
Russ	riff	crap	frock	gram		raft	scrimp
		crop			grasp	rift	script
		crud	frill	trot	grump		sprint
		crab	frog	trod	grand	draft	
		crib		track	grant	drift	
		crack	press	trick	grunt		trust
		crick	prim	truck	graft		tramp
		crock	prom	tram			tromp
			prep	trim	brand	strand	trump
			prod	trap	brunt	strict	trend
			prick	trip	brisk	strum	tract
			prig	trek			

Appendix F

CVC				Consonant Blends	
van	jab	buzz *	hot	swim	went
vat	Jeb	fizz	hog	swig	wept
vet	Jeff	fuzz	hut	swell	welt
vim	job	Liz	had	twin	weld
Val	Jack	razz	hid	twig	
win	Jill		hub	twit	dwell
wet	jock	yes	huff	twist	yelp
wit	jig	yum!	hack	zest	hump
wed	jog	yen	heck	jest	hand
web	jug	yip	hick	just	hint
wick	jam	yet	hag	jump	hunt
wag		yuck!	hug	jilt	husk
wig	Jim	yell	hiss	vast	heft
well	Jan	yack	ham	vest	hilt
will	Jen		hem	vamp	helm
	jet	hat	him	vend	help
Zen	Jed	hit	hum	vent	held
zap!	jot	hell	hen	west	hulk
zip	jut	hill	hip	wisp	hasp
zit	jazz	hull	hop	wimp	hemp
zig-zag	jell			wind **	Swiss
Zack				wilt	swag
				wend	swept

* BUZZ is a CVC word because ZZ symbolizes a single sound: /z/.
** Pronounce this with a short I rather than a long I.

Note: Boxed words are important, high-frequency words.

S says /z/			
as	is	has	his

Some Anomalies					
QU = KW	**X = KS**		**WR = R**	**WH = W**	**KN = N**
quit	ox	sex	wrap	when?	knot
quiz	ax	six	wreck	whip	knack
quilt	box	lax	wrist	whim	knit
quick	fax	tax	wren	whiz	knob
quip	fix	wax		wham!	knock
quest	fox	pox		whiff	
quell	max	vex		whump	
quack	mix	flex		whap!	
squid	nix	text		whack!	
squint	sax	next		whisk	
squish	hex	tux			
	flax				

Appendix G

SH			CH			TH	
SH-	-SH	-SH	CH-	-TCH	-NCH	TH-	THR-
ship	ash	brush	chap	batch	inch	thus	throb
shop	cash	crash	chip	botch	bunch	that	thrift
shack	dash	crush	chop	catch	lunch	thump	thrill
shock	dish	fresh	check	ditch	hunch	theft	thrust
shed	fish	bash	chick	fetch	munch	thick	thrash
shall	gash	gush	chuck	hatch	pinch	thug	
shell	rash	hush	chill	latch	punch	them	
shin	lash	sham	chin	match	ranch	than	
shun	lush	brash	chat	pitch	stench	then	
shot	mash	Josh	chum	patch	branch	thin	
shut	mush		chest	stitch	brunch	thud	
shaft	sash	clash	champ	snatch	crunch	this	
shift	wish	flash	chimp		drench		
shelf	Welsh	flesh	chump	snitch	French	-TH	
	squish	flush	chant	sketch	quench	bath	
	hash	trash	chug	scratch	trench	Beth	
SHR-	gosh!	plush		crotch	scrunch	math	
shred	rush	slash	-CH	crutch	flinch	path	
shrub	stash	slush	much	itch	finch	wrath	
shrug	splash		such		wrench	with	
shrill	smash		rich	witch *		smith	
shrimp	blush		which *	Dutch		fifth	
			belch	blotch		sixth	
				clutch		tenth	
				glitch		broth	
				stretch		moth	
				notch		cloth	
				hutch		filth	
				etch		depth	
				wretch		width	

* Discuss the difference

Two Special Groups		Final S says /s/		Final S says /z/	
E/EE	**ALL**	snacks	nuts	cans	drums
be	all	hats	plants	balls	beds
he	ball	lips	tents	eggs	bugs
me	call	pets	pests	bells	stands
she	fall	chicks	gifts	hens	ends
we	hall	quits	fists	kids	pigs
see	mall	rocks	stamps	twigs	hands
three	tall	pots	bumps	thrills	shells
tree	stall	lamps	gulps	swims	smells
pee	wall	ducks	puffs	fins	runs
bee	small	helps	ships	cobs	webs
glee	squall	jumps	cups	nods	grins
knee		maps		sees	trees
fee				bags	tubs
flee				is	his
free				as	has
the **					

** Usually pronounced /TH/ + /u/

Appendix H

ING	ANG	UNG	ONG	ENG
king	bang	dung	long	length
ring	gang	hung	song	strength
sing	rang	sung	wrong	
wing	sang	flung	strong	
thing	slang	strung	throng	
fling	fang	stung	bong	
string	hang	lung	prong	
swing	pang	swung	gong	
bring	clang			

ING	ANK	INK	UNK	ONK
sting	bank	fink	bunk	bonk
sling	drank	blink	dunk	honk
ding	rank	brink	gunk	wonk
cling	sank	drink	junk	conk
ping	tank	kink	punk	plonk
wring	yank	link	sunk	
I sing.	thank	pink	chunk	
He sings.	blank	rink	stunk	
They sing.	crank	sink	trunk	
You sing.	prank	slink	clunk	
We sing.	spank	stink	drunk	
She sings.	stank	think	flunk	
my ring	dank	wink	hunk	
our ring	plank	ink		
your ring	flank	mink		
their ring				
her ring				
his ring				

Some decodable multi-syllable words

seven	consent	exist	liquid	present	sickness
eleven	backpack	fastest	magnet	punish	solid
belong	bandit	finish	mattress	puppet	sunset
nothing	banish	sandwich	melted	rabbit	talent
hundred	basket	gossip	muffin	rapid	radish
absent	biggest	habit	napkin	restful	chipmunk
fungus	British	hottest	panic	robin	vanish
difficult	bucket	illness	picnic	rocket	tennis
comet	cabin	insect	planet	rubbish	himself
elastic	Wisconsin	fragment	planted	sadness	expect
electric	often	limit	plastic	racket	address
blinking	chicken	event	pocket	visit	abolish
fantastic	combat	ticket	sinking	English	jacket
halibut	comment	timid	disrupt	bashful	invent
ketchup	complex	topic	banana	publish	diminish
minimum	contest	relax	basketball	children	selfish
maximum	cricket	drinking	benefit	splendid	begin
public	dentist	pumpkin	cabinet	tantrum	goblin
vivid	discuss	drumstick	dustpan	enchant	upset
lament	exit	disgust	bathtub	within	reckless

Adding ES creates a second syllable*			
box	boxes	glass	glasses
fox	foxes	branch	branches
dish	dishes	fizz	fizzes
wish	wishes	dress	dresses
brush	brushes	splash	splashes
flush	flushes	scratch	scratches
fix	fixes	catch	catches
kiss	kisses	bench	benches
crash	crashes	lunch	lunches
itch	itches	munch	munches

* The final S says /z/

Adding ING to words			
sit	sitting	kiss	kissing
dig	digging	wish	wishing
swim	swimming	fish	fishing
skip	skipping	thrill	thrilling
fib	fibbing	flush	flushing
run	running	plant	planting
jog	jogging	stand	standing
grin	grinning	grasp	grasping
drip	dripping	sketch	sketching
spit	spitting	belch	belching
chop	chopping	twist	twisting
fix **	fixing	pitch	pitching
mix	mixing	dump	dumping

** X is never doubled because it already stands for 2 consonants: KS.

Note: When adding ING, double a single consonant following the vowel. If you don't, the vowel becomes long (compare BIDDING and BIDING). You'll deal with long vowels shortly.

Appendix J
Long Vowels

			/A/			
bake	came	ale	crane	ape	ate	fade
make	game	bale	mane	gape	date	jade
lake	same	gale	pane	tape	fate	made
take	tame	male	sane	drape	hate	wade
snake	lame	pale	wane	grape	late	shade
quake	blame	sale	plane	escape	mate	blade
brake	flame	tale	Jane	shape	rate	glade
cake	shame	whale	insane	scrape	crate	trade
wake	name	stale	lane	cape	gate	grade
fake	became	scale			slate	spade
flake	frame	Yale	bare	Dave	state	
sake		exhale	dare	gave	plate	knave
shake	craze	female	fare	pave	skate	square
mistake	faze	inhale	mare	rave	Kate	
cupcake	gaze		rare	save		
	haze	chase	share	wave		
	maze	base	flare	shave	haste	
	raze	vase	glare	brave	waste	
	blaze	case	stare	grave	paste	
	glaze	erase	scare	slave	taste	
	graze		spare	behave		

			/E/			
here	Pete	theme	Steve	eve	these	Steven
complete	concrete	extreme	athlete	compete	fete	excrete
stampede	severe	crème	serene	impede		millipede

			/U/		
cube	cute	fume	cure	use	dispute
puke	mute	volume	pure	fuse	excuse
rebuke	refute	legume	secure	abuse	confuse
cupid	mule	compute	figure	muse	amuse

/I/

dime	hide	life	file	fire	bite	dive
lime	ride	rife	mile	tire	white	hive
mime	side	wife	pile	wire	kite	jive
time	tide	strife	tile	shire	mite	live
chime	wide	knife	vile	spire	rite	chive
grime	glide	fife	smile	ire	site	thrive
slime	bride		while	retire	trite	five
crime	pride	dine		hire	spite	drive
	stride	fine	pipe	admire	smite	
bike	slide	line	ripe	desire	quite	prize
dike	divide	mine	wipe	inspire	write	size
hike	inside	nine	gripe			wise *
like		pine	swipe			rise *
Mike	tribe	wine	snipe	strike		
pike	scribe	vine	stripe	spine		
spike	bribe	shine				
dislike	describe	swine				

* A final S can have a Z sound

/O/

joke	dome	abode	tote	bone	cope	rose
poke	home	code	wrote	cone	mope	chose
woke	Rome	mode	smote	hone	dope	hose
yoke		node	dote	tone	hope	close
spoke	dole	rode	quote	clone	pope	doze
bloke	hole		vote	drone	rope	froze
choke	mole			scone	scope	pose
broke	pole	cove	lobe	stone	slope	suppose
smoke	role	stove	globe	throne	grope	nose
stoke	sole	drove	robe		trope	oppose
stroke	stole	trove	strobe			those
	whole	rove	probe			

Appendix K
Long Vowels

/O/		/E/					
OA		**EE**			**EA**		
boat	hoax	deed	steel	steer	bead	jeans	seat
float	coax	feed	kneel	queer	lead	lean	cheat
goat	load	heed	eel	sneer	plead	mean	treat
coat	road	need	beef	peer	read	clean	each
gloat	toad	seed	reef	beet	knead	bean	beach
bloat	moat	bleed	beep	feet	leak	cheap	peach
cloak	oath	breed	deep	meet	beak	leap	reach
soak	coach	creed	keep	sweet	bleak	ear	teach
oak	roach	freed	peep	sheet	speak	dear	heap
oat	poach	greed	seep	fleet	squeak	fear	feast
goal	topcoat	speed	weep	tweet	deal	smear	peak
coal	unload	weed	sheep	greet	heal	gear	weak
foam	croak	meek	steep	sleet	meal	near	sneak
loam	toasting	seek	sleep	street	real	rear	tea
roam	loafing	week	creep	keen	seal	tear	sea
loan	throat	sleek	beer	teeth	steal	clear	pea
moan	toast	creek	deer	green	squeal	hear	beast
groan	roast	feel	jeer	seen	beam	year	least
oar	coast	heel	leer	teen	cream	wheat	yeast
roar	boast	keel	cheer	queen	team	eat	east
soar	oaf	wheel	squeeze	peek	dream	beat	season
soap	loaf	peel	freeze	cheek	gleam	neat	reason
		jeep	breeze	sweep	steam	defeat	oatmeal
		deem	sneeze	Greek	stream	heat	seacoast
		seem	geese	degree	scream	meat	ease *
		teem	cheese *	sleeve	heave	grease	tease *
					leave	release	please *
					weave	increase	decrease

* A final S can have a Z sound

/A/

AI

raid	rain	stair	trail	quaint	affair
afraid	vain	fair	flail	saint	detail
laid	chain	hair	quail	paint	attain
paid	train	lair	jail	pigtail	raisin
braid	sprain	pair	mail	bait	sailboat
aid	drain	chair	nail	wait	obtain
maid	brain	flair	pail	strait	refrain
repaid	strain	air	rail	trait	explain
gain	stain	ail	frail	remain	complain
lain	Spain	snail	hail	aim	railroad
slain	plain	fail	waist	maim	maintain
main	grain	sail	faith	claim	raincoat
pain	again	tail	mailbox	repair	airline

16 EA exceptions		from
Short E	**Long A**	**Appendix G**
dead	bear	be
head	tear	we
bread	wear	me
instead	pear	he
read *	swear	she
threat	break	pee
sweat	steak	flee
meant	great	free
		tree
		see
		glee
		bee
		fee
		knee
		tee
		three

* Discuss the two pronunciations of this word

Adding S or ES		
likes	bites	needs
makes	prizes *	sleeps
grapes	chokes	peaches *
skates	ropes	cleans
saves	snores	beasts
bikes	dozes *	roaches *
hides	supposes *	seas
wipes	mules	trains
tires	uses *	flashes *

* Requires an extra syllable because the last sound in the original word is /s/, /z/, /ch/, or /sh/

Adding ING			
bake	baking	moan	moaning
take	taking	weep	weeping
skate	skating	toast	toasting
share	sharing	feed	feeding
bike	biking	speak	speaking
hike	hiking	dream	dreaming
ride	riding	rain	raining
slide	sliding	sail	sailing
smile	smiling	wear	wearing
bite	biting	pee	peeing
write	writing	see	seeing
behave	behaving	flee	fleeing
puke	puking	speed	speeding
rise	rising	soak	soaking

Appendix L
The Final 8 Vowel Sounds

/ew/					/oo/	/oy/	
OO		**EW**	**UE**	**U-E**	**OO**	**OY**	**OI**
moon	moo	blew	true	tube	took	boy	boil
soon	mood	chew	glue	nude	book	joy	soil
spoon	tooth	brew	flu	dude	hook	soy	coil
croon	booth	crew	Sue	prude	cook	toy	oil
goon	pool	dew	blue	rude	crook	coy	spoil
lagoon	poop	flew	due	include	brook	Roy	toil
loon	poor	grew	clue	Duke	shook	ploy	foil
noon	root	knew	untrue	Luke	nook	ahoy!	roil
balloon	scoop	new	avenue	fluke	look	annoy	broil
groom	shoot	stew	cruel	June	rook	enjoy	coin
boom	boot	threw		prune	good	busboy	join
doom	too	strew		tune	wood	convoy	groin
loom	tool	slew		dune	stood	decoy	loins
room	troop	Jew		flute	hood	destroy	poison
zoom	zoo	drew		brute	foot	employ	joint
broom	boo!	screw		salute	soot	loyal	point
food	hoof	news		costume	wool	royal	appoint
fool	raccoon	shrew		consume	**except**:	alloy	void
goo	bloom	lewd		pollute	flood	boycott	droid
goop	proof			crude	blood		avoid
hoop	gloom			lure			devoid
hoot	roof			conclude			hoist
loop	scoot		**/y/ = /ew/**				moist
loot	booty		few	rescue			foist
snoop	kook		tissue	value			exploit
buffoon	saloon	pooch	cure	volume			toilet
baboon	igloo	groove	fuel	cure			oink
goof	spook	ooze		pure			
boost	cool	choose		compute			
moose	goose	loose					

/ow/			/aw/		
OW	**OU**		**AW**	**AU**	**Other**
cow	round	out	jaw	haul	
bow	found	pout	raw	maul	**-ALT**
how?	ground	rout	saw	Paul	salt
now	hound	scout	law	laud	halt
vow	mound	shout	paw	fraud	malt
chow	pound	spout	flaw	fault	
brow	sound	stout	draw	vault	**-ALK**
plow	bound	trout	claw	taut	walk
wow!	wound	sprout	thaw	taunt	stalk
ow!	loud	lout	straw	haunt	talk
pow!	cloud	clout	slaw	jaunt	chalk
yow!	proud	devout	lawn	flaunt	
allow	count	about	pawn	aunt	
	mount	couch	yawn	daunt	**-ALL**
brown	fount	pouch	fawn	gaunt	ball
crown	south	grouch	dawn	launch	fall
down	mouth	slouch	crawl	haunch	all
drown	oust	crouch	brawl	exhaust	hall
frown	joust	ouch!	bawl	August	call
gown	roust	astound	shawl	sauna	tall
town	foul	around	sprawl	because *	small
clown	noun	amount	hawk	assault	wall
owl	our	discount	gawk	autumn **	stall
howl	sour		awful	augment	mall
growl	flour	**except:**	outlaw	applaud	
fowl	dour	group			
prowl	devour	soup			
cowboy		youth			
crowd					

* Not so tricky after all!
** Silent N prepares for "autumnal"

/ar/			/or/			
AR			**OR**			**ORE**
jar	farm	harp	or	orbit	actor	bore
far	fart	harsh	nor	stubborn	cantor	gore
arch	farther	lard	for	forget	captor	core
arm	hard	march	cord	port	condor	lore
art	harm	maroon	lord	minor	doctor	more
bar	lark	marsh	ford	major	horse	pore
barf	mark	park	dorm	worn	comfort	chore
bark	dart	part	form	moron	corncob	shore
barn	March	start	storm	effort	corner	sore
car	market	scarf	born	harbor	north	tore
card	cartoon	scarlet	corn	morning	forth	spore
cart	tar	shard	horn	sort	porch	wore
chard	target	shark	morn	short	scorch	store
charm	tart	sharp	torn	snort	color	snore
chart	yard	smart	thorn	airport	author	score
dark	yarn	spark	fort	formal	discord	explore
starch	harpoon	star	export	escort	absorb	before
apart	alarm	quart	import	New York	coral	ignore
snarl	carve	starve	valor	sailor	dork	adore
Carl			victor	pork	moral	implore
arc			sport	stork	gorilla	restore
arctic			scorn	savor	forest	
			organ	afford	orb	
			mortal	door *	cork	
				floor *	fork	
	except:			**except:**		
	war		word	worst	worm	
	warm		work	world		

* OOR is an uncommon spelling for /or/

/er/						
ER			**IR**		**UR**	
after	hotter	cover	smirk	dirt	turn	hurl
under	smaller	monster	squirm	first	burn	turd
never	bigger	oyster	chirp	whirl	spurn	surf
over	smarter	fern	birch	sir	burst	turf
her	softer	stern	birth	stir	church	curl
hers	faster	verb	girth	third	burp	burger
other *	taller	booger	mirth	thirst	slurp	curt
brother *	darker	finger	irk	girl	hurt	purse
mother *	harder	expert	shirk	skirt	blurt	blur
sister	liver	computer	shirt	squirt	lurk	slur
tower	butter	internet	quirk	flirt	curb	concur
shower	river	disaster	firm	bird	spurt	purr
flower	farmer	corner	direct	squirrel	lurch	fur
power	carpenter	silver	twirl	swirl	burner	churn
number	wonder	permanent			disturb	curve
perch	destroyer	term			survive	curse
asteroid	lever	September			cur	blurb
otter	perk	sneakers			suburb	burnt
herd	jerk	thunder			absurd	burden
nerd	clerk	tender			duress	unfurl
hunger	permit	blister			incur	nurse
dinner	insert	ladder			occur	current
twerp	verse	nerve			curtail	
perform	serve	observe				
toaster	barber	anger				
singer		thinker				

* The O in these 3 important words is closer to an /u/ sound.

Appendix M

/A/			/O/			
AY			**O**	**OW**		**OE**
away	pay	Norway	go	arrow	minnow	doe
bay	play	dismay	no	below	mow	foe
day	pray	betray	so	blow	narrow	hoe
decay	ray	saying	also	borrow	pillow	Joe
delay	runway	playing	pro	bow	row	toe
essay	say *	staying	metro	bowl	shadow	oboe
gay	slay	Monday	cargo	burrow	shallow	woe
gray	spray	Tuesday	jello	crow	show	goes
hay	birthday	Wednesday	hello	elbow	slow	
hurray!	stay	Thursday	loco	glow	snow	
yay!	stray	Friday	bingo	flow	sow	
lay	sway	Saturday	banjo	grow	sparrow	**except**:
may	today	Sunday	buffalo	grown	stow	shoe
nay	tray	okay	mango	hollow	swallow	canoe
May	way	blue jay	oregano	know	throw	
maybe	repay	clay	pesto	low	tow	
fray	layer	array	polo	mellow	widow	
subway	holiday	display	tempo	knows	willow	
			motto	own	window	
			torso	known	yellow	
			poncho	growing	billow	
			going	knowing	sorrow	
			jumbo	showing	bellow	
			condo	following	fellow	
			except:	snowing	follow	
			to			
			do			
			who			

* SAY is no longer a "tricky" word.

/I/		/E/				
Y	**IE**	**Y**			**EY**	**E/EE**
my	pie	belly	greedy	screwy	key	be
by	die	any	grouchy	silly	monkey	he
why?	lie	angry	grumpy	skinny	donkey	me
cry	tie	berry	hairy	sleepy	money	we
try		bloody	happy	stinky	honey	she
fly		bossy	hungry	snowy	valley	fee
fry		bumpy	injury	soapy	turkey	bee
shy		candy	itchy	softly	trolley	knee
sky		chewy	jelly	sorry	hockey	pee
sly		comedy	jolly	speedy	barley	see
spy		creamy	jumpy	starry	whiskey	flee
dry		creepy	kitty	sticky	kidney	glee
ply		curly	lousy	story	chimney	tree
spry		daddy	lucky	study	gooey	agree
guy *		daily	mainly	stuffy	parsley	three
buy *		dearly	many	sunny	alley	free
		dirty	mommy	thirsty	jockey	coffee
		easy	thirty	except:		toffee
		enemy	nasty	toasty		disagree
		every	nippy	tricky		degree
		fairly	noisy	tummy		employee
		family	party	ugly		foresee
		foggy	penny	very		referee
		funny	puppy	cloudy		
		fussy	rocky	yummy		
		fuzzy	rusty	forty		
		goofy	sadly	fifty		
					except:	
		except:			obey	
		July	defy	supply	prey	
		reply	deny	apply	grey	
			multiply		hey!	
					they	

* slightly irregular

Adding ING					
try	trying	dry	drying	hurry	hurrying
cry	crying	say	saying	play	playing
fly	flying	stay	staying	study	studying
fry	frying	stray	straying	annoy	annoying

Adding Y to a short vowel word			
sun	sunny	fish	fishy
fun	funny	rock	rocky
pig	piggy	smell	smelly
mom	mommy	stick	sticky
dad	daddy	slush	slushy
sex	sexy *	fuzz	fuzzy
fog	foggy	mess	messy
mug	muggy	hand	handy

* Never double X. It already represents KS.

Adding Y to a long vowel word			
shine	shiny	foam	foamy
smoke	smoky	soap	soapy
haze	hazy	toast	toasty
grime	grimy	weep	weepy
slime	slimy	sleep	sleepy
scare	scary	sneak	sneaky
shade	shady	rain	rainy

Adding LY to a word			
safely	widely	rudely	loosely
loudly	timely	lonely	bravely
lately	freely	likely	closely

Forming the Plural

Change Y to I and add ES				Simply add S			
candy	candies	dummy	dummies	pay	pays	annoy	annoys
belly	bellies	fifty	fifties	day	days	monkey	monkeys
story	stories	jelly	jellies	play	plays	turkey	turkeys
penny	pennies	body	bodies	pray	prays	kidney	kidneys
party	parties	bunny	bunnies	stay	stays	destroy	destroys
twenty	twenties	fly	flies	tray	trays	decay	decays
kitty	kitties	try	tries	boy	boys	delay	delays
guppy	guppies	cry	cries	toy	toys	spray	sprays

Lazy vowels defaulting to /u/

A = /u/			AL = "ULL"		EL = "ULL"	
panda	flora	abide	pedal	dismal	camel	channel
vanilla	about	adore	royal	mortal	tunnel	snorkel
extra	adapt	adult	animal	arrival	squirrel	gavel
zebra	adopt	agree	normal	comical	travel	rebel
Nebraska	aloof	avoid	dental	metal	vowel	barrel
alarm	apart	ajar	floral	central	towel	funnel
along	awake	alone	medical	survival	axel	gospel
adorn	abuse	aware	hospital	medal	chapel	marvel
amend	appoint	arrest	sandal	formal	novel	shovel
umbrella	momma	America	equal	signal	damsel	pretzel
afraid	attach	pizza *	festival	carnival	panel	hazel
acclaim	amaze	plaza	mental	loyal	nickel	level
annoy	parka	around	several	petal	grovel	vessel
arrive	soda	abort			morsel	tinsel

* very irregular!

Lazy vowels defaulting to /i/

cotton	Boston	kitten	shorten	payment	prudent
carton	bitten	listen	given	thousand	sudden
button	fasten	rotten	vixen	kitchen	skeleton
mountain	item	talent	pavement	student	atlas
fountain	enemy	element	absent	happen	lemon
focus	gallon	evident	garment	ribbon	pelican

Appendix N

The Giggle Group					
giggle	jiggle	drizzle	puddle	kettle	tinkle
apple	juggle	eagle	purple	kissable	example
babble	cuddle	fickle	puzzle	little	fizzle
battle	snuggle	fiddle	riddle	lovable	sniffle
beetle	needle	fixable	rubble	marble	startle
bottle	nibble	feeble	sample	middle	sizzle
bubble	doodle	wobble	gobble	mumble	humble
buckle	nipple	wiggle	handle	struggle	tumble
bumble	noodle	ankle	simple	tackle	uncle
bundle	nuzzle	possible	muffle	tattle	waffle
candle	battle	visible	mingle	temple	jungle
cattle	paddle	gargle	people *	terrible	huggable
chuckle	pebble	hassle	knuckle	tickle	huddle
cripple	pickle	poodle	crumble	saddle	topple

* Slightly irregular - just hide the O.

The GH Groups					
IGH = /I/		AUGH = /aw/	OUGH = /aw/	EIGH = /A/	GH = /f/
night	fright	caught	ought	eight	rough
light	delight	taught	bought	weight	tough
might	tonight	daughter	sought	freight	enough
right	high	naught	fought	sleigh	laugh
sight	thigh	fraught	thought	weigh	cough
tight	sigh	naughty	brought	neigh	
fight	nigh	haughty	wrought	neighbor	
slight	**except:**	distraught			
flight	bite				
bright	spite			**except:**	
plight	kite			height	

PH = /F/					
phone	humph!	Ralph	elephant	prophet	hyphen
phase	phew!	orphan	phantom	triumph	pamphlet
oomph!	graph	telephone	nephew	Philip	sphere
phooey!	dolphin	alphabet	emphasis	phrase	phonics

The Wild Group			
IND	**ILD**	**OST**	**OLD**
bind	mild	most	old
find	wild	ghost	cold
mind	child	post	fold
blind		host	hold
grind			sold
wind			told
kind			gold
behind			scold
			bold

TION = "SHIN"		TURE = "CHER"	
action	direction	rupture	mixture
mention	caution	nurture	lecture
fiction	portion	fixture	texture
fraction	election	capture	fracture
addition	condition	posture	literature
subtraction	infection	pasture	vulture
multiplication	attention	culture	rapture
question *	tradition	picture	stature
ambition	invention	feature	creature
section	suction	mature	moisture
affection	adoption	venture	overture
option	audition	puncture	furniture
edition		departure	adventure
connection		signature	sculpture

* "CHIN" rather than "SHIN"

First Syllable Closed

din/ner	com/plete	des/cribe	mis/lead	im/press
sup/per	prob/lem	des/pise	sub/ject	in/sult
lad/der	com/mon	des/pair	sub/way	in/sist
dus/ty	per/haps	per/fect	sub/mit	in/spect
trav/el	dif/fer/ent	thir/teen	dis/as/ter	in/stinct
chil/dren	ex/am/ple	or/bit	fan/tas/tic	fif/ty
hel/lo	en/ter/tain	ov/en	dis/like	un/kind
nap/kin	hun/dred	emp/ty	dis/cuss	un/like
mis/ter	loud/ly	pub/lish	dis/rupt	un/do
con/test	dis/tant	in/spire	dis/pute	con/tain
trum/pet	con/stant	sep/ar/ate	dis/gust	kin/der/gar/ten
tun/nel	div/ide	en/joy/ment	dis/turb	in/ter/es/ting
les/son	sub/tract	his/tor/y	bur/den	un/der/stand
nev/er	fes/tiv/al	val/en/tine	fig/ment	but/ter/fly
bet/ter	ad/ven/ture	fing/er	com/ment	hos/pit/al
mom/my	im/por/tant	sup/pose	com/et	ill/ness
dad/dy	how/ev/er	bot/tom	sing/ing	dis/cov/er
hap/pen	sev/er/al	straw/ber/ry	num/ber	vow/el

First Syllable Open

la/dy	po/ta/to	na/ture	cre/a/tion	pi/lot
la/zy	ba/sic	mo/tion	ro/ta/tion	fla/vor
la/ter	hu/man	sta/tion	re/peat	bo/nus
ti/ny	pre/pare	va/ca/tion	be/tween	fi/nal
o/pen	pre/tend	na/tion	re/lax	be/hind
pa/per	pre/dict	lo/tion	u/nit	e/qual
pro/vide	re/lax	vi/bra/tion	u/nite	fa/tal
tu/lip	re/fute	e/mo/tion	o/dor	re/quire
so/lar	no/ble	tri/umph	e/vil	to/ma/to
pho/to	de/ny	re/mark	i/vy	re/mind
de/pend	de/coy	be/yond	ba/con	fre/quent
de/sire	de/lay	re/main	gra/vy	be/neath
to/tal	ta/ble	mo/ment	i/tem	re/quest
ri/val	ho/tel	thou/sand	ma/ple	e/qua/tor

Mixed Syllables

vol/ca/no	ex/act/ly
e/lec/tric	in/for/ma/tion
mel/o/dy	ev/er/y/one
an/at/o/my	de/jec/ted
Hal/lo/ween	dis/be/lief
ar/gu/ment	un/der/wear
choc/o/late	e/quip/ment
co/op/er/ate	in/ves/tig/a/tion
e/vap/or/ate	con/grat/u/la/tions
in/stru/ment	op/por/tu/nit/y
rep/re/sent	vo/cab/u/lar/y
pre/ven/tion	al/lig/a/tor
cu/cum/ber	com/mu/nit/y
re/mem/ber	con/stel/la/tion
par/tic/u/lar	ca/lam/it/y
tem/per/a/ture	con/stip/a/tion
lo/co/mo/tive	Oc/to/ber
cal/cu/la/tor	No/vem/ber
ed/u/ca/tion	ap/pli/ca/tion
ev/er/y/thing	dic/tion/ar/y
con/so/nant	con/sti/pa/tion

Appendix O

Y = /I/			Y = /i/		
style	hyphen	tyke	crystal	lyrics	syllable
type	hydrant	tyrant	cryptic	myth	synthetic
hype	dynamic	hybrid	nymph	mystery	system
analyze	dynasty	dynamite	syrup	oxygen	symptom
hyena	python	hyper	lynx	rhythm	symbol
typhoon	nylon	hydrate	lynch	physics	hypnotize
tycoon	pylon	typhoid	lymph	typical	

S can spell /z/					
nose	abuse	pause	use	is	whose
rise	cause	suppose	his	refuse	these
hose	tease	expose	as	always	please
rose	close	compose	was	those	has
wise	accuse	praise	does	chose	choose
pose	oppose	cheese	goes	dispose	raise
prose	advise	excuse	says	disclose	enclose

C can spell /s/ (Soft C)					
ice	race	circle	certain	since	reduce
nice	pace	citrus	cents	wince	produce
rice	space	city	succeed	mince	decide
spice	face	cycle	ceremony	sentence	mercy
twice	lace	cyan	fascinate	princess	exercise
vice	place	cell	icy	recess	lettuce
dice	grace	celebrate	spicy	except	literacy
mice	embrace	cigar	fancy	bounce	pencil
lice	accent	cymbal	Nancy	pounce	sauce
price	celery	cynic	dance	notice	December
slice	cement	cyclone	glance	choice	simplicity
ace	center	cider	chance	rejoice	service
brace	concentrate	circus	prince	cylinder	force
cereal	magnificent	central	process	faucet	peace
	necessary	exciting	absence	fence	

G can spell /j/ (Soft G)

age	huge	large	college
cage	refuge	charge	courage
page	merge	orange	manage
rage	emerge	gym	sausage
sage	range	gyp	lounge
stage	change	gypsy	sponge
wage	strange	rigid	ginger
image	urge	gender	Ginny
engage	purge	gin	gel
package	virgin	urgent	gently
garbage	verge	general	original
damage	fudge	gentle	gesture
passage	judge	gem	gigantic
average	grudge	germ	giant
cabbage	nudge	gene	allergy
village	edge	gibberish	tragic
voyage	pledge	energy	logic
savage	ledge	stingy	imagination
luggage	dodge	apology	refrigerator
advantage	lodge	magic	intelligent
digit	badge	gyrate	Egypt
agile	agenda	agitate	emergency

except:			
gill	gift	get	give
girl	giggle	gimmick	

Silent E categories				
A	**B**	**C**	**D**	**E**
home	nice	stage	pickle	have
mistake	space	image	noodle	give
five	embrace	damage	struggle	move
mule	chance	huge	rattle	love
arrive	prince	change	snuggle	above
case	choice	fudge	rubble	delve
wise	spice	manage	bottle	glove
sale	disgrace	sponge	drizzle	nerve
Steve	sauce	orange	purple	reserve
game	fence	college	temple	involve
time	practice	garage	terrible	resolve
F	**G**	**H**	**I**	
true	house	breeze	climate	
blue	mouse *	sneeze	private	
due	moose	are	accurate	
clue	goose *	one	deliberate	
glue	horse	were	delicate	
recue	corpse	awe	opposite	
subdue	nurse	come	definite	
tissue	spouse	some	estimate	
avenue	curse	done	volatile	
argue	eclipse	giraffe	chorale	
continue	promise	else	literate	

* The plural, of course, is mice and geese

IE and EI both spell /E/				
IE		**EI**	**diminutives**	**plurals**
grief	cookie	receive	doggie	sixties
thief	movie	conceive	Mollie	ladies
chief	believe	deceive	Tommie	armies
brief	relieve	receipt	Maggie	babies
belief	achieve	perceive	Susie	cookies
relief	piece	conceit	Katie	bodies
field	niece	ceiling	oldie	bunnies
yield	shriek	either	softie	pennies
shield	fiend	neither	kiddie	goodies
wield	cashier	leisure	cutie	candies
hygiene		seize		
		weird		
		caffeine		
		deceit		
		sheik		
		protein		
except:				
stein	reign	friend	their *	vein
veil	view	heir	feint	

* An earlier tricky word

33 Common Contractions		
Contraction	**Short for**	**Phonetic**
aren't	are not	ARNT
can't	can not	CANT
couldn't	could not	COODINT
didn't	did not	DIDINT
doesn't	does not	DUZINT
don't	do not	DOANT
hasn't	has not	HAZINT
haven't	have not	HAVINT
he'll	he will	HEEL
he's	he is	HEEZ
I'll	I will	ILE
I'm	I am	IME
isn't	is not	IZINT
it's	it is	ITS
I've	I have	IVE
let's	let us	LETS
she'll	she will	SHEEL
she's	she is	SHEEZ
shouldn't	should not	SHOODINT
they'll	they will	THAIL
they're	they are	THAIR
they've	they have	THAVE
wasn't	was not	WUZINT
we'll	we will	WEEL
we're	we are	WEER
weren't	were not	WERNT
we've	we have	WEEV
who's	who is	HOOZ
won't	will not	WOANT
wouldn't	would not	WOODINT
you'll	you will	YOOL
you're	you are	YOOR
you've	you have	YOOV

Appendix P
The Code: Spelling
(Encoding Sounds into Letters)

	Sound	Possible Letters			
1	/A/	a-e* (made)	ai (sail)	ay (stay)	a (nation)
		ea (great)	eigh (eight)	ey (they)	ei (vein)
2	/a/	a (hat)			
3	/E/	ee (week)	ea (heat)	y (candy)	ie (field)
		e (me)	ei (receive)	e-e* (theme)	ey (key)
4	/e/	e (bed)	ea (bread)	ai (said)	
5	/I/	i-e* (time)	i (tiny)	y (cry)	igh (high)
		ie (pie)			
6	/i/	i (sit)	y (myth)		
7	/O/	o-e* (hope)	oa (boat)	o (go)	ow (snow)
		oe (toe)	ough (though)		
8	/o/	o (got)	a (father)		
9	/u/	u (nut)	oo (blood)	o (from)	oe (does)
		ou (rough)			
10	/ew/	oo (moon)	ew (grew)	u-e* (prune)	ue (blue)
		u (student)	o (do)	ui (fruit)	oe (shoe)
		ou (you)	ough (through)		
11	/oo/	oo (book)	u (pull)	ou (could)	
12	/oy/	oi (soil)	oy (joy)		
13	/ow/	ou (loud)	ow (cow)		
14	/aw/	au (fraud)	aw (lawn)	a (ball)	o (dog)
		augh (taught)	ough (bought)		
15	/ar/	ar (car)			
16	/or/	or (corn)	ore (store)	our (four)	oor (door)
17	/er/	er (perch)	ir (birch)	ur (church)	ure (treasure)

* The hyphen stands for any consonant

	Sound	Possible Letters			
18	/b/	b (bat)			
19	/d/	d (dog)	dd (add)		
20	/f/	f (fun)	ph (phone)	ff (stuff)	gh (rough)
21	/g/	g (gift)	gu (guest)	gh (ghost)	gg (egg)
22	/h/	h (happy)			
23	/j/	j (jar)	g (germ)		
24	/k/	k (keep)	c (cat)	ck (pick)	ch (school)
25	/l/	l (lake)	ll (bell)		
26	/m/	m (man)			
27	/n/	n (net)	kn (knife)	gn (gnat)	
28	/p/	p (past)			
29	/r/	r (run)	wr (write)		
30	/s/	s (sleep)	c (city)	ss (kiss)	
31	/t/	t (top)	ed (picked)	tt (mutt)	
32	/v/	v (van)	f (of)		
33	/w/	w (wish)	wh (white)		
34	/y/	y (yellow)			
35	/z/	z (zipper)	s (hands)	zz (jazz)	
36	/sh/	sh (ship)	t (action)	s (mission)	c (special)
37	/SH/ *	s (vision)	z (seizure)		
38	/ch/	ch (chin)	t (nature)		
39	/th/	th (thank)			
40	/TH/ *	th (mother)			
41	/ng/	ng (sing)			

* Voiced version of the sound (see Chapter 2)

Appendix Q
The Code: Reading
(Decoding Letters into Sounds)

Letter	Possible Sounds			
a	/a/ (apple)	/A/ (paper)	/aw/ (ball)	
b	/b/ (boy)			
c	/k/ (cat)	/s/ (city)	/sh/ (precious)	
d	/d/ (dog)			
e	/e/ (enemy)	/E/ (me)		
f	/f/ (fan)	/v/ (of)		
g	/g/ (get)	/j/ (energy)		
h	/h/ (hat)			
i	/i/ (in)	/I/ (title)	/E/ (stadium)	
j	/j/ (jam)			
k	/k/ (kiss)			
l	/l/ (lip)			
m	/m/ (mat)			
n	/n/ (nap)			
o	/o/ (box)	/O/ (bonus)	/aw/ (dog)	/ew/ (do)
p	/p/ (pickle)			
qu	/k/+/w/ (quit)			
r	/r/ (run)			
s	/s/ (sit)	/z/ (pans)	/sh/ (tension)	/SH/ (vision)
t	/t/ (top)	/ch/ (future)	/sh/ (action)	
u	/u/ (up)	/y/+/ew/ (cube)	/ew/ (rude)	/oo/ (pull)
v	/v/ (van)			
w	/w/ (win)			
x	/k/+/s/ (box)			
y	/y/ (yell)	/E/ (candy)	/I/ (fly)	/i/ (myth)
z	/z/ (zip)	/SH/ (seizure)		

Letters	Possible Sounds		
ai	/A/ (sail)	/e/ (said)	
ar	/ar/ (far)		
au	/aw/ (fraud)		
aw	/aw/ (lawn)		
ay	/A/ (pay)		
ch	/ch/ (chip)	/k/ (school)	
ck	/k/ (stick)		
dd	/d/ (add)		
ea	/E/ (seat)	/e/ (head)	/A/ (great)
ed	/d/ (called)	/t/ (picked)	
ee	/E/ (keep)		
ei	/E/ (receive)	/A/ (vein)	
er	/er/ (her)		
ew	/ew/ (new)	/y/+/ew/ (few)	
ey	/E/ (key)	/A/ (they)	
ff	/f/ (stiff)		
gg	/g/ (egg)		
gh	/g/ (ghost)	/f/ (laugh)	
gn	/n/ (gnat)		
ie	/E/ (brief)	/I/ (pie)	
ir	/er/ (dirt)		
kn	/n/ (knee)		
ll	/l/ (bell)		
ng	/ng/ (sing)		
nk	/ng/+/k/ (sink)		
oa	/O/ (boat)		
oe	/O/ (toe)	/ew/ (shoe)	/u/ (does)
oi	/oy/ (boil)		
oo	/ew/ (moon)	/oo/ (good)	/u/ (blood)
or	/or/ (corn)		
ore	/or/ (store)		

Letters	Possible Sounds		
oor	/or/ (door)		
ou	/ow/ (cloud)	/oo/ (could)	/ew/ (you)
ow	/ow/ (cow)	/O/ (snow)	
oy	/oy/ (toy)		
ph	/f/ (phone)		
ps	/s/ (psychic)		
sh	/sh/ (ship)		
ss	/s/ (mess)		
th	/th/ (thin)	/TH/ (these)	
tt	/t/ (mutt)		
ue	/ew/ (blue)	/y/+/ew/ (cue)	
ui	/ew/ (fruit)	/i/ (build)	
ur	/er/ (church)		
wh	/w/ (when)		
wr	/r/ (wrist)		
zz	/z/ (jazz)		

Letters	Possible Sounds		
a-e*	/A/ (bake)		
e-e*	/E/ (theme)		
i-e*	/I/ (time)		
o-e*	/O/ (stone)		
u-e*	/ew/ (tune)	/y/ + /ew/ (cute)	
augh	/aw/ (caught)		
eigh	/A/ (eight)	/I/ (height)	
igh	/I/ (right)		
ough	/aw/ (thought)	/O/ (though)	/ew/ (through)

* The hyphen stands for any consonant

The following common letter strings are phonetically irregular. The beginning reader should master these 14 pronunciations. Many of these are good examples of Lazy Vowel (see Stage 14).

Letters	Possible Sounds	
-ind	/I/ + nd (find)	/i/ + nd (wind)
-ild	/I/ + ld (child)	/i/ + ld (build)
-ost	/O/ + st (most)	/o/ + st (lost)
-old	/O/ + ld (cold)	
-le	"ull" (bubble)	
-ous	"iss" (joyous)	
-ious	/E/ + "iss" (curious)	
-cious	"shiss" (precious)	
-tion	"shin" (fraction)	
-sion	"shin" (mission)	/SH/ + "in" (vision)
-sure	"sher" (pressure)	/SH/+/er/ (measure)
-ture	"cher" (future)	
-cial	"shull" (facial)	
-tial	"shull" (partial)	

Appendix R
The Consonant Blends

31 Beginning Blends			45 Ending Blends		
bl	pl	spl	ct	mp	rb
br	pr	spr	dth	mpt	rd
cl	sc	shr	ft	nth	rf
cr	sk	sph	fth	nch	rg
dr	sl	squ	x = ks	nk	rk
dw	sm	str	lt	nt	rl
fl	sn	tr	lf	nd	rm
fr	sp	tw	lm	ngth	rn
gl	sw	thr	ln	pth	rp
gr	st	scr	lth	pt	rt
	qu = kw		lp	tch	rch
			lsh	xt	rsh
			ld	sp	rth
			lk	st	rve
			lch	sk	rst

Appendix S
The Tricky 50

Correct Spelling	Phonetic Spelling	Correct Spelling	Phonetic Spelling
above	abuv	said	sed
are	ar	says	sez
because	becuz	should	shood
been	bin	some	sum
come	cum	sure	shoor
could	cood	their	thair
do	doo	there	thair
does	duz	they	thay
done	dun	though	tho
eight	ate	through	throo
eye	I	to	too
four	for	two	too
friend	frend	want	wunt
from	frum	was	wuz
give	giv	watch	wawch
goes	goze	water	wawder
gone	gawn	were	wer
have	hav	what	wut
love	luv	where	wair
move	moov	who	hoo
of	uv	whose	hooz
once	wuns	woman	woomin
one	wun	would	wood
only	oanly	you	yoo
put	poot	your	yoor

In the above phonetic spellings, OO sometimes spells /oo/ and sometimes spells /ew/, just as it does in GOOD FOOD.

Appendix T

EU = /ew/		or	EU = /y/ + /ew/	
eulogy	neuter	feud	leukemia	queue
eunuch	neuron	sleuth	deuce	eureka!
		pseudo		

IO	EO	IU	UA	UI	IA	
lion	eon	opium	usual	ruin	friar	mania
radio	video	odium	dual	fluid	liar	via
riot	rodeo	sodium	actual *	truism	dial	petunia
idiot	meow	podium	jaguar	bruin	trial	giant
audio	peony	medium	sexual	suicide	vial	Maria
scorpion	peon	radius	truant	intuit	denial	dialog
biopsy	yeoman	genius	ritual *	genuine	jovial	piano
axiom	meteor	helium	nuance	tuition	trivial	aviation
ravioli	stereo	calcium	mutual *	penguin	material	utopia
violin	nucleon	premium	sensual		maniac	pliable
biology	galleon	aquarium	gradual	fruit	fiasco	diatribe
carrion	jeopardy	stadium	factual *	juice	phobia	amphibian
champion	theology	delirium	virtual *	suit	diary	burial
chariot	surgeon	tedium	punctual	bruise	media	medial
Ohio	dungeon	geranium	annual	cruise	anemia	menial
studio	theorem	aluminum	casual	recruit	diagram	median
cardio	geometry	gymnasium	persuade		diamond	alias
violent	luncheon		language	guide	diaper	pariah
million	deodorant		valuable	guess	Georgia	bacteria
onion				guilt	genial	Louisiana
opinion				guitar	bias	California
union				guile	avian	aviator
region				disguise	familiar	deviate
				guest	diagonal	brilliant

* The T has a /ch/ sound, as in Stage 16

Forming the Past Tense					
Add D		**Add ED**		**Double the Consonant**	
smile	smiled	play	played	beg	begged
love	loved	stay	stayed	wag	wagged
close	closed	enter	entered	tag	tagged
pee	peed	scream	screamed	grin	grinned
use	used	snow	snowed	jog	jogged
die	died	plow	plowed	grab	grabbed
lie	lied	rain	rained	brag	bragged
share	shared	foam	foamed	rub	rubbed
behave	behaved	moan	moaned	fib	fibbed
dine	dined	jeer	jeered	pin	pinned
describe	described	cheer	cheered	rob	robbed
snore	snored	dream	dreamed	drum	drummed
chuckle	chuckled	clean	cleaned	hum	hummed
giggle	giggled	boil	boiled	stun	stunned
		join	joined		
ED says /t/		**2 Syllables**		**Change Y to I, add ED**	
flush	flushed	nod	nodded	carry	carried
kiss	kissed	wait	waited	hurry	hurried
check	checked	skate	skated	cry	cried
sip	sipped	chat	chatted	fry	fried
laugh	laughed	float	floated	try	tried
fish	fished	melt	melted	copy	copied
pinch	pinched	end	ended	envy	envied
leak	leaked	wilt	wilted	bully	bullied
splash	splashed	yield	yielded	empty	emptied
soak	soaked	fade	faded	marry	married
skip	skipped	trade	traded	tarry	tarried
sniff	sniffed	taste	tasted	scurry	scurried
cough	coughed	waste	wasted	worry	worried
bake	baked	toast	toasted	stymy	stymied
chase	chased	greet	greeted	reply	replied
look	looked	shout	shouted		
crash	crashed				

Comparative and Superlative

hot	hotter	hottest	shady	shadier	shadiest
tall	taller	tallest	sunny	sunnier	sunniest
smart	smarter	smartest	dirty	dirtier	dirtiest
soft	softer	softest	messy	messier	messiest
small	smaller	smallest	hard	harder	hardest
wet	wetter	wettest	easy	easier	easiest
ripe	riper	ripest	brave	braver	bravest
sweet	sweeter	sweetest	cheap	cheaper	cheapest

The OUS Family

OUS = "iss"	IOUS = /E/ + "iss"	UOUS = /U/ + "iss"	CIOUS = "shiss"
joyous	curious	strenuous	vicious
enormous	previous	arduous	gracious
nervous	serious	incongruous	luscious
jealous	obvious	conspicuous	precious
famous	envious	continuous	spacious
scandalous	various	fatuous	atrocious
fabulous	hilarious	ingenuous	conscious
dangerous	furious	innocuous	delicious
numerous	tedious	sensuous	ferocious
ravenous	odious	sumptuous	malicious
hazardous	studious	virtuous	pernicious
poisonous	victorious	voluptuous	suspicious
generous	hideous	ambiguous	
odorous	nefarious		
perilous	notorious		
rigorous	glorious		
barbarous	copious		
zealous	spurious		
callous	delirious		
pompous	dubious		
raucous	melodious		
gorgeous	devious		

In 2 of these 5 word groups, the 41st (and final) sound of English finally appears. It's the *voiced* version of /sh/, symbolically, /SH/.

SION = "shin"	SION = /SH/ + "in"	SURE = /SH/ + "er"	CIAL = "shull"	TIAL = "shull"
tension	vision *	measure *	facial	partial
mansion	decision *	treasure *	racial	martial
pension	collision *	pleasure *	social	spatial
mission	version *	closure *	crucial	essential
session	illusion *	leisure *	glacial	potential
passion	division *	exposure *	special	torrential
omission	explosion *	composure *	official	initial
expansion	occasion *	fissure *	financial	credential
admission	confusion *	seizure *	artificial	prudential
expression	conclusion *			
compassion	invasion *			
permission	aversion *			
	fusion *			
	erosion *			

* The S in these words has the same sound
as the S in the word ASIA

The Mute Group					
mute B	**mute C**	**mute G**	**mute H**	**mute K**	**mute L**
bomb	scissors	sign	ache	knew	half
comb	science *	assign	chaos	knave	calf
dumb	ascend	design	Christmas	knee	folk
doubt	descend	gnat	character	knife	yolk
lamb	scent	gnaw	chord	knit	caulk
thumb	scene	gnarly	echo	knob	
crumb	muscle	gnash	orchid	knock	
climb	scintillate	cologne	school	knuckle	
numb	czar	gnome	ghost	knight	
mute N	**mute P**	**mute S**	**mute T**	**mute W**	
autumn	psalm	aisle	castle	wrap	
solemn	pseudo	debris	fasten	wrath	
column	psych	island	hustle	wreck	
condemn	pneumonia	isle	listen	answer	
damn	coup	Illinois	moisten	wretch	
hymn	raspberry		nestle	wrist	
	cupboard		whistle	wrong	
	receipt		wrestle	sword	
			jostle	two	

Appendix U
The 100 Most Frequent Words

Rank	Word	Rank	Word	Rank	Word	Rank	Word	Rank	Word
1	the	21	this	41	so	61	people	81	back
2	be	22	but	42	up	62	into	82	after
3	to	23	his	43	out	63	year	83	use
4	of	24	by	44	if	64	your	84	two
5	and	25	from	45	about	65	good	85	how
6	a	26	they	46	who	66	some	86	our
7	in	27	we	47	get	67	could	87	work
8	that	28	say	48	which	68	them	88	first
9	have	29	her	49	go	69	see	89	well
10	I	30	she	50	me	70	other	90	way
11	it	31	or	51	when	71	than	91	even
12	for	32	an	52	make	72	then	92	new
13	not	33	will	53	can	73	now	93	want
14	on	34	my	54	like	74	look	94	because
15	with	35	one	55	time	75	only	95	any
16	he	36	all	56	no	76	come	96	these
17	as	37	would	57	just	77	its	97	give
18	you	38	there	58	him	78	over	98	day
19	do	39	their	59	know	79	think	99	most
20	at	40	what	60	take	80	also	100	us

Source: Concise Oxford English Dictionary (11th edition, 2006).

Given the phonics presented in this program, only the boxed words could be considered slightly irregular.

Bibliography

Adams, Marilyn Jager. *Beginning to Read: Thinking and Learning about Print.* Cambridge: MIT Press, 1990.

Beck, Isabel. *Making Sense of Phonics.* New York: The Guilford Press, 2006.

Calkins, Lucy. *The Art of Teaching Reading.* New York: Addison-Wesley, 2001.

Calkins, Lucy. *The Art of Teaching Writing.* Portsmouth: Heinemann, 1994.

Chall, Jeanne. *Learning to Read: The Great Debate.* Updated ed. New York: McGraw-Hill, 1967.

Dehaene, Stanislas. *Reading in the Brain: The New Science of How We Read.* New York: Penguin Books, 2009.

Ehri, Linnea. "Grapheme-Phoneme Knowledge is Essential for Learning to Read Words in English." In *Word Recognition in Beginning Literacy,* edited by Jamie Metsala and Linnea Ehri, 3-40. Mahwah, NJ: Lawrence Erlbaum Associates, 1998.

Eide, Denise. *Uncovering the Logic of English: A Common-Sense Approach to Reading, Spelling, and Literacy.* Minneapolis: Pedia Learning, 2012.

Fassett, James. *The New Beacon Primer.* New York: Ginn and Company, 1921.

Flesch, Rudolf. *Why Johnny Can't Read.* New York: Harper & Row, 1955.

Flesch, Rudolf. *Why Johnny Still Can't Read.* New York: Harper & Row, 1981.

Fox, Barbara. *Word Identification Strategies: Building Phonics into a Classroom Reading Program.* Upper Saddle River, NJ: Pearson Education, 2006.

Gaskins, Irene. "Procedures for Word Learning: Making Discoveries about Words." *Reading Teacher* 50 (1996): 312-27.

Gates, Arthur. "Studies of Phonetic Training in Beginning Reading." *Journal of Educational Psychology* 18 (1927): 52-69.

Goodman, Ken. *What's Whole in Whole Language.* Portsmouth: Heinemann Educational Books, 1986.

Goodman, Ken. "Reading: A Psycholinguistic Guessing Game." *Journal of the Reading Specialist,* May (1967): 120-37.

Heilman, Arthur. *Phonics in Proper Perspective.* Upper Saddle River, NJ: Pearson Education, 2006.

Huey, Edmund. *The Psychology and Pedagogy of Reading.* 1908. Reprint: Cambridge: M.I.T. Press, 1968.

Lemann, Nicholas. "The Reading Wars." *The Atlantic,* November (1997): 80-6.

Liberman, I. Y. and Liberman, A. M. "Whole Language vs. Code Emphasis: Underlying Assumptions and Their Implications for Reading Instruction." *Annals of Dyslexia* 40 (1989): 181-94.

McGuinness, Diane. *Why Our Children Can't Read: And What We Can Do About It.* New York: Simon & Schuster, 1997.

McGuinness, Diane. *Growing a Reader from Birth: Your Child's Path from Language to Literacy.* New York: W. W. Norton & Company, 2004.

Medina, John. *Brain Rules for Baby: How to Raise a Smart and Happy Child from Zero to Five.* Seattle, Pear Press, 2010.

Milton, James and Jeanine Treffers-Daller. "Vocabulary Size Revisited: The Link Between Vocabulary Size and Academic Achievement." *Applied Linguistics Review* 4.1 (2013): 151-172.

Owens, Robert. *Language Development: An Introduction.* Boston: Pearson Publishing, 2005.

Pinker, Steven. *The Language Instinct.* New York: William Morrow, 1994.

Pressley, Michael. *Reading Instruction That Works: The Case for Balanced Literacy.* New York: Guilford Press, 2006.

Rigney, Daniel. *The Matthew Effect: How Advantage Begets Further Advantage.* New York: Columbia University Press, 2010.

Shaywitz, Sally. *Overcoming Dyslexia.* New York: Alfred Knopf, 2004.

Smith, Frank. *Reading Without Nonsense.* 3 ed. New York: Teachers College Press, 1997.

Sprenger, Marilee. *Wiring the Brain for Reading: Brain-Based Strategies for Teaching Literacy.* San Francisco, John Wiley & Sons, 2013.

Stamm, Jill. *Bright from the Start.* New York: Penguin Group, 2007.

Wolf, Maryanne. *Proust and the Squid: The Story and Science of the Reading Brain.* New York: HarperCollins, 2007.

Web Sites

"Adult Literacy in America," 3rd ed., National Center for Educational Statistics, U.S. Department of Education, April 2002. <https://nces.ed.gov/pubs93/93275.pdf> (Accessed 14 Sept 2017).

"The Nation's Report Card," National Assessment of Educational Progress, 2015. <https://www.nationsreportcard.gov/reading_math_2015/#reading?grade=4> (Accessed 14 Sept 2017).

"Media and Young Minds," American Academy of Pediatrics, October, 2016. <http://pediatrics.aappublications.org/content/early/2016/10/19/peds.2016 -2591> (Accessed 14 Sept 2017).

Report of the National Reading Panel, *Teaching Children to Read: An Evidence-Based Assessment of the Scientific Research Literature on Reading and Its Implications for Reading Instruction.* https://www.nichd.nih.gov/publications/pubs/nrp/documents/report.pdf (Accessed 14 Sept 2017).

59278777R00126

Made in the USA
Columbia, SC
01 June 2019